"One of the great casualties of the latter part of the 20th century is the death of dreamers. The society has startling statistics on the increase of crime; the increase of mental and emotional breakdowns; the increase of wrecked marriages; but there are no statistics about the alarming number of men and women living without dreams. Reverend William Campbell takes on this very important issue with prophetic clarity. Those in the Christian community are aware that present day problems can be solved by ancient solutions. What this evangelist has done is lift the Word of God as the solution for those living with broken dreams. Minister Campbell does a masterful job in exegeting the Word of God in such a manner that the biblical solutions will be clear to everyone who reads this outstanding work. If you are ready to dream again—open the pages of this book."

*Bishop John R. Bryant*
*African Methodist Episcopal Church*

---

"In an age where many people are disillusioned because of broken . . . shattered . . . aborted . . . or deferred dreams, it is refreshing to read a book that offers hope, encouragement, and promise. Reverend Campbell provides a fresh insight on this divinely inspired topic. The book is based on biblical principles which assure the reader that God-given dreams do come true! This book is a must for those who know they have a purpose and a destiny to fulfill."

*Bishop George D. McKinney, Ph.D.*
*Chu*

D1275012

"*Born to Dream* is a book that every visionary should read. This book will not only encourage but enlighten individuals who are destined to work in ministry. When you read these pages, allow the anointing of the Holy Spirit to work in your life. Allow your visions and dreams to be birthed. The experience of God's power will develop a miraculous work of God to enhance the building of God's Kingdom."

*Pastor Danny R. Poe*
*African Methodist Episcopal Church*

# BORN TO DREAM

William M. Campbell, Jr.

Born to Dream
by William M. Campbell, Jr.

ISBN  1-58169-009-6
For Worldwide Distribution
Printed in the U.S.A.

Second Printing: January, 2003

Gazelle Press
An Imprint of Genesis Communications, Inc.
P.O. Box 91011 • Mobile, AL 36691
(888) 670-7463

# DEDICATION

To the memory of the greatest earthly father I know—
Reverend William Melvin Campbell, Sr.
Thank you for teaching me how to hold on
to my dreams. Thank you for my spiritual inheritance.

# ACKNOWLEDGMENTS

My father always said that salvation is the *process of becoming.* I am thankful for those who have contributed to the success of my spiritual journey. For the completion of this project, there were some very special people who helped me in some very special ways.

A prominent note of thanks to Pastor and Mrs. Larry L. Carther and my family at Faith Center For All Nations. Your gift of hospitality is not to be compared. A very special "thank you" goes to the following for believing and investing in the project during its conception stage: Bishop and Mrs. John R. Bryant; Pastor J.L. Butler, Upperroom Christian Faith Center; Rev. Rudolph P. Gibbs, Sr., Ebenezer A.M.E. Church; Bishop Wesley Tunstall, Mount Moriah Christian Church; Rev. Irene M. Campbell, Rescue House of Prayer; Bishop Wayne L. Johnson, Bibleway Deliverance Center; Dr. Detroit R. Williams, Williams Temple, C.O.G.I.C.; and Rev. Lucius Williams, Crossroads of Life.

# TABLE OF CONTENTS

# INTRODUCTION

It was the blizzard of 1996. Pastor Larry L. Carther welcomed me to Faith Center For All Nations in Muncie, Indiana. The opening sermon, "The Price of Dreaming," was the message the Lord told me I would be preaching.

That Sunday morning in the services, the Lord spoke a prophetic word to the church. From that moment, I knew that the meeting was going to be unusual. Testimonies are still ringing from what the Lord did in what became a two-week revival. Hundreds were touched! Many received healing and miracles! For 13 nights, the people of God (blacks and whites, Methodists, Baptists, Apostolics, and others) came together for a move of God. So rich was the experience that the Lord instructed me to "write this vision and make it plain." What was previously just 13 sermons is now 13 chapters of one of my greatest experiences of the *rhema*—utterance—of God.

I encourage you to read Genesis 37-50 before you begin this book. By reading these Scriptures first, you will have a fuller, richer revelation experience. In your reading, my prayer is that you will discover that you were born to dream!

## Chapter One
# The Price of Dreaming

*And Joseph dreamed a dream, and he told it his brethren: and they hated him yet the more.* (Genesis 37:5).

Throughout the ages, God has provided humanity with those who have vision and insight into the future: those who have unusual gifts that can cause catalytic events to reshape man's destiny and direction; vessels who are possessed of uncommon spirit, who can move the masses to new levels of awareness and activity. These men and women have done wondrous things. They have invented machines, discovered cures for diseases and composed words which have moved people to action. They have entertained, taught and changed the course of history. Other significant, and in some cases cataclysmic, events have also been found in the wake of their presence. In spite of their gifts, which have benefitted many people, every one of these visionaries has paid an incredible price to be the unique vessel of grace God has destined each of them to be.

Dreamers are typically very unique people. They generally don't associate with crowds, and they always seem to have something to do. They are often quite eccentric in their behavior, although they generally never intend to offend anyone with their intense preoccupation for accomplishing what is locked inside their heads and hearts. When they dream, usually their dreams (as the Lord would have it) encompass not only their own interests, but also the concerns and needs of those around them. In spite of this resumé, which obviously supports them as a necessary part of the community, ironically they are often the most criticized, despised, misunderstood and ostracized members of our society. Yet, a true dreamer has one characteristic that defies logic and confounds their detractors: they are willing to pay the price to make their dreams become reality. Joseph, the son of Jacob, was such a man—a dreamer.

> *For God speaketh once, yea twice, yet man perceiveth it not. In a dream, in a vision of the night, when deep sleep falleth upon men, in slumberings upon the bed; Then he openeth the ears of men, and sealeth their instruction, that he may withdraw man from his purpose, and hide pride from man* (Job 33:14-17).

Dreams are the God-inspired visions through which God emblazons His divine purpose upon the heart of a man or woman. In our dreams, God finds a way to communicate with us, especially when we don't find time to talk with Him. In our sleep, when we are at rest, God can communicate His divine purpose to our spirits. He "seals" His instruction within us to "withdraw" us from our own purposes and to lead us in His way—the way of humble service.

Sometimes dreams are the only way God can

communicate with us. During the daytime we are too busy working in order to pay the bills, going to the grocery store or mall, making dinner or washing the clothes. We don't keep our communication lines open with Him, because we're just "too busy." God can't get a word in "edgewise." So we see that God can, and does, often speak to us through dreams to make His will known to us.

*And it shall come to pass afterward, that I will pour out my spirit upon all flesh; and your sons and your daughters shall prophesy, your old men shall dream dreams, your young men shall see visions* (Joel 2:28).

God can do whatever He wants. Therefore, He can speak to any of us through dreams, visions or prophesies to give us timely, specific directions to keep us within His perfect will for us.

After a night of sleeping and dreaming, the dreamer wakes up and goes about his or her daily tasks. At this point, there is no conflict: the challenge comes to the dreamer when he or she attempts to *do* what they have dreamed about. At this juncture, many lose heart, afraid to act on their dreams or visions. We are fundamentally afraid to venture into the unknown. But if God is leading us, what He is asking us to do is definitely worth the risk.

The following is one of my trademark sayings. The first two lines are not mine originally, and I do not know where they came from. The rest of the statement is from my own experience and helps us see the inspiration we need to have in order to progress:

If you always *do* what you have always done,
You will always have what you always had.
If you always *go* where you have always gone,
You will always be where you have always been.
If you always *see* what you have always seen,
You will always know what you have always known.
If you always *give* what you have always given,
You will always reap what you have always reaped.
Give nothing, then reap nothing.
See nothing, then know nothing.
Go nowhere, then be nowhere.
Do nothing, then have nothing.

Joseph was the well-favored son of Jacob the patri-arch. His father especially liked him because he was the son of his old age. His mother, Rachel, was the woman Jacob had wanted to marry and so had worked a total of 14 years in Padaranam to obtain her father's consent. Through his uncle Laban's trickery, Jacob was given her sister, Leah, on his wedding night after his first seven years of labor. Being drunk from the celebration, he did not realize who was sleeping in his tent until the morning. In spite of this setback, Jacob worked another seven years for Laban to secure Rachel in marriage. When Rachel finally conceived, Jacob's eleventh son, Joseph, was born.

Joseph, like his father, Jacob, his grandfather, Isaac, and his great-grandfather, Abraham, before him, had the gift of dreams. Dreaming was one of the ways God com-municated with them. It should not have been a surprise to Jacob that one of his sons would have that gift. He should have been looking for that spiritual blessing to come through one of his offspring. Jacob mistakenly did not support Joseph's gift. When Joseph's older brothers envied their father's affection for him, Jacob could have helped to neutralize the situation and promote good relations within the family. Jacob, however, took a passive role, choosing to *observe* the gift rather than *protect* it for the benefit of the entire family. This passivity later would come back to haunt Jacob. Joseph's apparent demise shocked Jacob into over-protecting his youngest son, Benjamin.

The Jacobs of our day need to be on guard to protect our Josephs. Too often we let valuable, anointed men and women, boys and girls fall prey to the envy and spite of the world. Joseph's brothers hated Joseph because they could not define and understand their own gifts and talents. His gifting and anointing were openly displayed before them, whereas they had nothing to boast about.

Making matters worse, Joseph always seemed to know how please his father. He always knew the right words to say and the best way to carry off an event. He appeared to be getting what they were not receiving.

There are at least four things that every human being needs: acceptance, affection, approval and attention. Joseph seemed to be getting all of these things from his father; meanwhile, his brothers felt they were less important and neglected. As a result, they felt justified in removing him from the family.

Dreamers are thrown into pits and disposed of every day because they dare to set the tone and direction for others, venturing to tell their brothers and sisters what they must do to make a difference in the world. Dreamers are killed every day because they have the courage to share their vision to build great ministries and churches, their dreams beyond the comprehension of their contemporaries. Because they see things on a different level, their dreams are subject to attack at any moment. As one great church leader told me, "If you bring that vision here, they will kill your vision and steal your dream."

Envy and anger keep many believers grounded who could otherwise soar in the Spirit. Their attacks are not personal, though they may make them such. Their grudge is with God, who has chosen to bless others. Dreamers need to take steps to protect their dreams. As a pastor friend of mine, Floyd Flake, once said, "You must fly so high they can only stab your feet; you may be limping, but they won't have stabbed you in your *heart* (where you love God) or your *head* (where His vision is communicated), because these are kept out of reach."

Dreamers pay a heavy price just to make the world better for themselves and for those around them. In the end, however, it is well worth the dream, not for the pleasure of saying, "I told you so," but for the real joy in seeing the benefits of their dream shared—not only with those who love them, but also with those who may have doubted, envied, hated, condemned, despised, criticized or rebuked them.

## Chapter Two
# Never Stop Dreaming

*And when they saw him afar off, even before he came near unto them, they conspired against him to slay him. And they said one to another, Behold, this dreamer cometh. Come now therefore, and let us slay him, and cast him into some pit, and we will say, Some evil beast hath devoured him: and we shall see what will become of his dreams* (Genesis 37:18-20).

There are four gifts or facets in every organization that are essential for the effective accomplishment of a vision. First, there are those who are "dreamers"—the "idea people"—responsible for generating ideas that lead to effective actions being taken. These are the people who have vision about what can be done.

Second, we have the "dream developers," or those who can get an idea "off of the ground" and make it "take on a life of its own." When they hear what the plan is, they immediately put their talents and gifts to work for the accomplishment of the vision. They are the launchers who get the work going.

Next, we have the "dream managers," or those who

can "keep it running." They do not attempt to change what God has given; instead, they keep it going just as they were instructed. Following orders is not a weakness, but a strength. These people are the ones who maintain the charted course.

Fourth, we have the "dream evaluators," or those who help others to see the beauty of the vision God has given and how each one must work together for its accomplishment. These are the people who like to have appreciation services for the pastor and others who have toiled for the working out of the vision.

Many times in an organization, we miss the beauty of the complete picture of what we can be and do together. Oftentimes we lose the benefit of what each of the four gifts bring to the whole. Like Joseph's brothers, envy and hatred can blind our eyes from seeing the value of our own roles, and hence the value of others' contributions as well. When we do not understand our value, we will see others as being of little or no value at all to the work.

Many of us are angry with God and do not know it. We are upset with Him because He has gifted others with abilities that we desire but do not possess. We covet others' God-given gifts at the tragic expense of not recognizing our own. This envy, based on hatred, is dangerous and should not be present among the body of believers. All too often this dangerous extension of the worldly perspective impedes the progress of the vision that God desires to bring to pass in the work of the ministry. Envy is a work of the flesh (Galatians 5:21). It is an uncontrolled desire to have or possess the things or abilities of another. Often it is confused with jealousy, which is born out of love.

God Himself states that He is "a jealous God" (Numbers 20:5). He does not like it when His people give praise to another. Much in the same way, a husband does not like his wife to give too much credit to another man, or vice versa.

Many, however, confuse envy with jealousy. Envy "rots the bones" (Proverbs 14:30), but jealousy spurs one on to do better for the one they are jealous over. Envy is promoted by hatred, while jealousy is born out of love. If you say you love your brother or sister, there is no way that you should be envious of them, for your love will help you to see their importance to the work of God. If you are envious, you will despise those who appear to be accomplishing more than you, and those who receive more attention, affection and approval than you. Envy will make you lash out at those you think are doing more than what you are doing. Jesus helped us by giving us a commandment to combat the envy to which we are susceptible.

*Again, a new commandment I write unto you, which thing is true in him and in you: because the darkness is past, and the true light now shineth. He that saith he is in the light, and hateth his brother, is in darkness even until now. He that loveth his brother abideth in the light, and there is none occasion of stumbling in him. But he that hateth his brother is in darkness, and walketh in darkness, and knoweth not whither he goeth, because that darkness hath blinded his eyes. . . . We know that we have passed from death unto life, because we love the brethren. He that loveth not his brother abideth in death. Whosoever hateth his brother is a murderer: and ye know that no murderer hath eternal life abiding in him. Hereby perceive we the love of God, because He laid down His life for us: and we ought to lay down our lives for the brethren* (I John 2:8-11; 3:14-16).

When we allow God to move in us, He will cause our dreams to come to pass; and we will not have time to envy others for their dreams, because we will be too busy fulfilling God's command for ours. Unfulfilled people spend most of their times *watching* what dreamers are *doing*. Being too much a spectator in life wastes time for the development of our own dreams and delays the purpose of God from being accomplished in our lives. We have heard it said, "Great people talk about *ideas*; average people talk about *things*; small people talk about *other people*."

When we allow God to move in us and accomplish His dream for our lives, we will learn to appreciate what He does in others, because we will also realize what we can and cannot accomplish by ourselves. We will appreciate the contributions of others because we will know that their contributions complement and add to our own. Our desire will be satisfied when we see the *whole* program come to fulfillment, and not just the part we played in it.

## Chapter Three
# Dreams Never Die

*And it came to pass, when Joseph was come unto
his brethren, that they stript Joseph out of his coat,
his coat of many colours that was on him; And they
took him, and cast him into a pit: and the pit was
empty, there was no water in it* (Genesis 37:23-24).

Jesus says that the words that He speaks are *"spirit
and life"* (John 6:63). Since God's words are "spirit," or
eternal, they never die. Before God spoke, He had a
thought or an idea. He framed that idea by speaking His
mind: *"And God said . . . and there was. . . ."* (Genesis
1:3). His words or ideas framed what He wanted to come
into existence (Hebrews 11:3). He will not change the
thing that has come out of His mouth, for it is the expression of His thoughts. All of His creation is *"upheld by the
word of His power"* (Hebrews 1:3).

When God gives you a dream, His instruction, sealed
within your spirit (Job 33:14-17), cannot be altered, for it
is the expression of God's thoughts for your life. Many
times you doubt from the dream (word of instruction)
because of circumstances and obstacles you encounter.
That is what the "pit" can do to you.

It is the inherent nature of man to resist the spiritual commandment of God, especially when it calls for the manifestation of a new thing that man is not used to. Many a man and woman have forfeited their God-given dreams because they were seeing something they had never seen before. They feared the criticism and ridicule they would experience from those around them if they attempted to act upon them. The vision, word, or dream of God is not subject to your environment, and most times it intentionally runs contrary to the *modus operandi* (mode of operation) of those around you so that God may be glorified when His will is accomplished in you. God likes to defy our human understanding and the critics by doing the thing in you that no one but you believes can be done.

The first key is the most important: God has to have *given you the dream.* Dreamers pay an incredible, or very credible, price first of all for *dreaming,* and then for *believing* in their dream. So the second key in order for your dream to come true is that you have to believe it, *even if no one else does.* By strengthening us through overcoming opposition, God prepares us for the greater blessing that He intends to bestow upon us—the reward of the faithful. This reward requires us to move out beyond what we have known, into the place that He will lead us to if we are willing. Placed in a position of uncertainty, we become uncomfortable and often feel as though God is not at all in the plan.

Others, who do not know where God has brought you in the Spirit in your personal walk with Him, do not know what God's will is for you; they can only advise you according to what He has shown them. They may think

12

that you need to be where they are, perhaps in a similar ministry, because that vision is the one that has been revealed to them as good and trustworthy. Therefore, friends, so-called advisors, family members and even spiritual leaders may try to discourage or inhibit your dream or vision according to what *they* think is best for you. They will give you well-intentioned advice based on *their* experience, which will make you feel that you are running counter to God's program as they know it to be.

Now, in the accomplishment of your dream, it is not necessary to argue with those whom you love, nor is it appropriate to disrespect the spiritual authority that God has placed over you. It is your responsibility to be subject to this authority. However, if the Lord has put His hand upon you to do a particular thing, you must acknowledge your authority and share with them your dream. If they embrace it, then God will direct them on how your dream may be accomplished. If they do not embrace it, then God will direct you in the ways in which your dream can be launched.

The keys to the success of your dream are: 1) *He gave it,* and 2) *you believe it.* If these two ingredients exist, then your dream will surely come to pass. If He gave you a vision, those who are spiritual will discern it and confirm it. Caution is needed, however, because everyone whom you might think to be in a position to interpret dreams may not be anointed for such an evaluation.

Nevertheless, just like the "certain man [who] found Joseph" (Genesis 37:15), God will send you a "certain" person, even while you are wandering in doubt and wondering if your vision is what God wants you to do.

Sometimes this type of situation is just the test to see if you are really *willing* to move into the realm of trust necessary for you to accomplish what God has told you to do. One of the first barriers to overcome when it is time for the dream or direction to be manifested is *you*. Many times you think that the will of God is some "far away thing" that you must work toward. Yes, after He has revealed what He wants you to do, you must "study to show yourself approved" (II Timothy 2:15) so that you may be prepared for the task. After the *preparation* (which, incidentally, we are always involved in), you must *perform*: you must do the thing that God has purposed for you to do.

God led me in faith and trust in an unpredictable situation when I attended the Florida Democratic Convention in Miami Beach, Florida, in December of 1995. To begin with, I took Interstate 275 via the Skyway Bridge in St. Petersburg in order to make my flight from Tampa to Miami. After paying the toll of one dollar, I had $15 remaining in my pocket.

Upon my arrival at the Miami airport, I went to the hotel phone bank to inquire about a free shuttle to their location. The hotel representative informed me the shuttle ran frequently and could be met immediately outside of the exit door. In closing the conversation, I stated the specific name of the hotel I was looking for. She said, "No, this is the airport hotel; what you want is the same hotel on Miami Beach." She also informed me that the taxi fare (no free shuttle) was $25.

Well, no problem. I needed $10 plus tip, and I could obtain that from an ATM machine using my VISA card.

Problem! I didn't know the PIN or access code. I had recently requested a form to change my PIN code, and although I could give the company the name of my grandmother's pet fish, they would not release my pin code over the phone. "No problem," I said to myself. "I can use my mobile phone and call some friends to come and pick me up." So, I dialed their numbers from memory. "At the tone, please leave a message and we will get back to you," was the voice message on the other end—all of my friends were at work and could not be reached in the middle of the day.

After allowing my bags to circle several times on the airport conveyor belt, I decided to retrieve them and sit down on my suitcase. Upon sitting down, I looked across the airport lobby to spot a telephone bank with yellow page directories hanging below them. If I could get across to the telephones, I could call some of my friends at work. Problem! I have all of these bags, and I am in Miami. If I call the skycap to help move me, he is going to expect $5 of the $15 I had left. If I leave them while I go to make the phone call, they may be "lifted up"—but not caught up with the Lord.

Just then, a young man on his lunch break came and sat at the counter behind me to enjoy his lunch. I asked him if he could watch the bags I left while I transported the rest of them across the room. He agreed. I stood up and picked up my bags—garment bag on one shoulder and laptop computer bag on the other, ministry case in one hand and briefcase in the other. Then to get it out of the way, I kicked the tape box. When I kicked it, it slid with ease. So I kicked it again and again and again, until

I had finally kicked and slid it all the way across the lobby. People were doing what you may be doing right now: *laughing!* But that is one of the properties of active faith: it looks foolish but it will get you where you need to go.

When I got across the lobby, I dropped my bags and looked out of the window. There was a transportation stand with a price list on the back of it. It read, "taxis— zone 4— Fountainbleau Hilton—$23"; "vans"—zone 4— Fountainbleau Hilton—$13." With $15 in my pocket, I could ride the van and still have enough left over for an order of fries and a Coke. I thought to myself, *Where do I catch the van?*

At that moment, a big airport van drove by. Using my mobile phone, I dialed the number on the side of the van. I said, "Hello, where do I catch your van?" The operator replied, "Just go out of the door and turn right; we are the next station down. By the way, where are you going?" I responded, "I am going to the Fountainbleau Hilton." "That will be $10," was the reply.

By riding the van, I could save $5 and have enough for the #2 meal at McDonald's, and I can even "super-size" it! When I was boarding the van ten minutes later, I sat and looked at a sign on the wall of the van. It read, "We accept VISA and Mastercard." I could keep my $15 in my pocket and use my "plastic power."

Just then, the Holy Spirit quickened a tremendous revelation in my spirit. Tears burst into my eyes, and I rejoiced all the way to the hotel. The Spirit whispered to me these words: "I give miracles to men who are in motion. When you move, you see. You don't see first and then move." Money was not what I needed: I needed information. The more I moved in faith, the more I saw and heard.

Ten men came to Jesus one day (Luke 17:12). They were sick with a disease called leprosy. It was the kind of disease where, while sleeping, one of your fingers could just drop off. They came to Jesus and asked Him to heal them. Jesus responded: "Go and show yourselves to the priest" (Luke 17:14a). *Go! Get in motion!* The Scripture then records that as they "went," they were healed (Luke 17:14b). Why? Because God gives miracles to those who are in motion. The fulfillment of your dream comes not in the talking of it, but in the *doing* of it! After you *hear* His voice, get in motion to *do* the work.

> *The word of the LORD came unto me, saying, Before I formed thee in the belly I knew thee; and before thou camest forth out of the womb I sanctified thee, and I ordained thee a prophet unto the nations. Then said I, Ah, Lord GOD! behold, I cannot speak: for I am a child. But the LORD said unto me, Say not, I am a child: for thou shalt go to all that I shall send thee, and whatsoever I command thee thou shalt speak* (Jeremiah 1:4-7).

Two of the most common excuses that people offer to God for not doing what He wants are age and inexperience. Like Jeremiah, you may feel inadequate when God calls for you to serve Him. This reaction is *natural*, but that is the problem: it's not the *spiritual* answer that God is looking for. God's response to Jeremiah's statement of inadequacy is "Say not" that you are incapable, for He is more than able.

By now, however, God was used to this type of resistance. He received the same type of answer from Abraham, Moses, Isaiah, Deborah, Peter and others. God is accustomed to our "natural" responses; that is why He sent the Holy Ghost to dwell within us to teach us how to give Him the spiritual response that will allow Him to move on with His purpose for our lives.

Examples of these excuses throughout the Bible include the following: 1) In Genesis 17:17, Abraham said, "My wife and I are old"; 2) In Exodus 4, Moses said, "I can't talk"; 3) In Isaiah 6, Isaiah tells God, "My lips are unclean"; 4) In Judges 4, Deborah responds, "I am a woman"; 5) In Jeremiah 1, Jeremiah says, "I am a child"; 6) In Acts 10, in the vision of unclean animals, Peter objects, "I am a Jew"; and 7) Paul says in II Corinthians 12:7, "I have a thorn."

These seemingly justifiable human limitations are self-imposed; God ignores and works around them. The purpose or dream of God is *not limited* by our own human weaknesses and conditions. It is in these conditions that He is *glorified*.

The dream or seed of greatness that God has placed within you will make you great. It is the thought of God for you expressed to you, so that you may be lifted up into His divine spiritual purpose. It is the noblest of experiences for your life after salvation, for it gives you divine spiritual direction that is flawless and allows you to take a glimpse into the future. It is a  precious divine revelation of the Spirit: *it never dies!* The words that Jesus speaks to us are "Spirit," and they are "life."

With anger raging in their hearts, Joseph's brothers plotted against him. Though some were overcome with hatred and envy, Reuben was able to buffer their violent emotion so as not to let it lead to Joseph's death. While deliberating about what they would do to this dreamer, Joseph's brothers threw him into a pit. Judah, the fourth son of Jacob, planned to come back and get Joseph out of the pit secretly; but before he could, a band of Midianite merchantmen came and got Joseph out. They, in turn, sold him to the Ishmaelites, who then sold him to the Egyptians. God pinned the outcome of Joseph on his brothers, because it was in their heart to do harm to him. *"As a man thinketh in his heart, so is he"* (Psalms 23:7).

God gave Joseph a supernatural dream and brought it to fulfillment. This fact is evident to us now, because we see the end result of the experience. But what about Joseph's feelings in exile and in prison, before his dream came to pass? Wouldn't they be much like our own? Do you think that Joseph felt abandoned by God, who had given him his dream? Do you think that he had to be thinking twice about whether God had really spoken to him? He must have had his share of doubts and complaints. He was human, *just like you and me.* That is what the pit, as well as envious brothers, will do to you—make you question and want to give up—testing your mettle to the limit. But remember, when God gives you a dream, your dream *never* dies! Hold on until He brings it to pass, and He will provide.

## Chapter Four
# From Pit To Prison:
# The Dream Lives On

*And Joseph was brought down to Egypt; and Potiphar, an officer of Pharaoh, captain of the guard, an Egyptian bought him of the hands of the Ishmaelites, which had brought him down thither. And the Lord was with Joseph, and he was a prosperous man; and he was in the house of his master the Egyptian . . . . And Joseph's master took him, and put him into the prison, a place where the king's prisoners* were *bound: and he was there in the prison. But the Lord was with Joseph, and shewed him mercy, and gave him favour in the sight of the keeper of the prison* (Genesis 39:1-2,20-21).

In Genesis 39:1-23, Joseph was brought down to Egypt. Potiphar, an officer of Pharaoh, captain of the guard and an Egyptian, bought him from the Ishmaelites. Since the Lord was with Joseph, He blessed everything Joseph did, and Potiphar made him the overseer of his house. It would have seemed that all was well, but Potiphar's wife desired Joseph and wore him down with temptations, day after day. Joseph eventually had to flee from her, naked, when there was no other way to escape. In order to protect herself, and possibly out of spite, she lied about Joseph to get him in trouble. Her husband put Joseph in prison; but even there, the Lord was with Him, had mercy upon him and gave him favor in the eyes of the warden, who placed all the prisoners in his care. Whatever went on in the prison, Joseph took care of it. The warden didn't have to worry about anything that Joseph was in charge of, since God prospered everything he did.

Many times, our perception of the will of God is that everything will be easy for us and will not require any significant effort on our part. We believe that God will not lead us anywhere that will put too much of a strain on us or take us out of the routine of our lifestyle.

But whereas God tells us we will not be tested beyond our endurance, it is obvious that God allows His true followers to be stretched to their limits. Jesus did say to love God "with all our strength" (Luke 10:27), and our calling will require just that. In Psalms 22:15, which relates to Jesus, the suffering servant, the Word says, *"My strength is dried up like a potsherd."* Suffering for our redemption deprived Jesus of all His strength. But God is glorified through our weakness, "For when we are weak, He is strong" (I Corinthians 4:10).

As we mature, He seems to allow more and more difficulties to come our way. As we learn to overcome them, He increases our ability to endure. He stretches us so that He can do more with us. He also sustains us so that we don't fall into sin. As tempted as Joseph must have been to sin by laying with Potiphar's wife, he never broke his

21

relationship with God, but he grew in strength and wisdom. Contrary to our liking, God's will is always direct-
ing us to *grow* by doing something we have *never done
before*, thus breaking our molded or "moldy" habits,
which can inhibit the free flow of God's Spirit in our
lives. When God has given a dream to us, the accomplishment of it will not always be *comfortable*, nor will it
always prove to be *convenient*. To make matters worse,
many whom we associate with and trust will try to influ-
ence us to take the "easy way out," when His purpose for
us may not allow that luxury of escape. We cannot allow
ourselves to be spun around and lose our peace, but must
continue to focus on God, who is in control of our lives.

Those who serve the Lord have to make significant
changes in their lifestyle in order to embrace God's will.
In order to receive the blessing of God, Abraham at the
age of 75 had to leave his family in Haran (Genesis
28:10). Later on, at the age of 137— after seeing the birth
of his son of promise, Isaac—Abraham had to obey the
Lord when He asked him to sacrifice his only son on an
altar (Genesis 22:2). God looked at his obedience and
knew that He could trust him with the greater blessing of
perpetual generations and an eternal inheritance (Genesis
22:16-18). We often cannot see the end result of things
God is asking us to do. We simply do not know what character and virtues God is forming in us by causing us to tri-
umph in difficult or seemingly impossible circumstances.

Daniel probably never thought that he would be
thrown into the lion's den (Daniel 6:16). After all, he was
a ranking political figure in the Babylonian kingdom. But
God was using this experience to prove His faithfulness

to Daniel and His power to Daniel's peers, who despised Daniel for his commitment to his dream.

Joshua's second battle, after the great victory at Jericho, ended up in defeat with 36 people out of 3,000 being killed. Joshua had to turn to the Lord, who showed him the remedy for the situation (Joshua 7:5-15).

David was anointed of the Lord to be king, but had to run from the anger of Saul for nearly ten years, waiting for his dream to come to pass. Saul threw javelins at him, hunted him down with a band of men and sent him out to battle, hoping he would be killed—just to keep David's dream (God's will) from being fulfilled in his life (I Samuel 18-28).

Jeremiah had to go through the spirit-breaking experience of being thrown into a pit where there was no light or food. From a pit with mire, leeches and disease, God brought him forth to fulfill His purpose in him. Not only was he thrown into a pit, but he had to completely rewrite his book of prophecy, which had been burned by those who despised him for the Word—the *dream* he believed in and spoke out with courage (Jeremiah 18:20;36:26).

The three Hebrew boys followed their dream. What did they end up with? A barbecue where they were not only the invited guests but the meat to be roasted. They saw what it was like to follow their dream through to completion, and God delivered them from their envious oppressors (Daniel 3:19-30). These and many others suffered uncomfortable and inhumane conditions, just because they dared to believe their dream and hold onto God's promise for them.

When God has entrusted you with the dream for your

life, you will have to go through refining experiences to prepare you for the performance of the dream and its benefits. The saying, "half the fun of arriving is getting there," will help you relate to the obstacles and opposition that you will encounter while on your way to fulfilling your dream. You wouldn't say it was enjoyable, but the "pit to prison" experience will yield you many jewels of wisdom and understanding that will help you to appreciate and maintain the blessings into which the dream is bringing you. No, it is never easy when you are going through it. Being thrown into a pit by those you thought loved you, and being sold into slavery twice and cast into prison for something that you did not do, are never easy experiences. The Scriptures admonish us to "take it patiently" (I Peter 2:20) knowing that God is bringing us a reward for our sacrifice.

So the Lord was with Joseph even in the pit. The Midianites pulled him out and sold him to the Ishmaelites, who sold him to Pharaoh's captain, Potiphar. God was with him and even his new master saw His anointing upon him. When God is with you, even those that sell, buy and enslave you will recognize that God is in you when you remain committed to your dream.

When you are sold out to the dream, however, the devil also takes notice of your commitment. He will proceed to distract you from your dream with those things that are apparently most lacking in your life.

Joseph was a young single man in his early twenties. The devil noticed this and tempted him with the attraction that young men are usually interested in at that age: a woman. Potiphar's wife was a well-to-do housewife with little or no significant responsibilities. Joseph's anointing attracted her. That is a property of the anointing: it attracts others for various reasons. Those who are anointed of the Lord know that it is the Holy Spirit that makes them attractive, and that those who are drawn to them are in need of what the *Spirit* has given, not necessarily what individual vessels of the Spirit can supply them with. We must be careful not to look to *people* to supply all that we need, for God is our source.

God gave grace to help Joseph not make the mistake of focusing on the gift rather than the Gift-giver. But it was not by Joseph's own power that he escaped temptation; it was by God's grace that he had the ability to walk away from the lure the devil was using to tempt him. One of the significant aspects of moving toward your dream is that the closer you get to its fulfillment, the harder the enemy of your soul will work to derail you. The closer you get and the brighter the light that shines upon you, the more you will attract attention. Don't be deceived by a lot of attention. If your friends see the light, so do your enemies.

In the city where I formally resided, I was often on television and in the newspapers for various causes and events. Those that knew me often noted this fact to me as a compliment. I learned a good response to give those who approached me, having seen me in some form of the media. I responded to them with, "It is one of the hazards of my business." This statement turned a few heads, as I also informed them that, "Not only do my friends—like you—see me, but so do my enemies."

Even in this injustice, the Lord was with Joseph and

showed him mercy by giving him favor with the prison keeper. Although in prison, his gifts continued to manifest themselves. No matter where God puts you, He has placed something inside of you that will be a blessing to those around you. Use your God-given gift to glorify God, and He will prosper you in your circumstance. From the pit to the prison, the dream *lives on*. Keep the dream alive!

## Chapter Five
# Born to Dream

*For whom he did foreknow, he also did predestinate to be conformed to the image of his Son, that he might be the firstborn among many brethren. Moreover whom he did predestinate, them he also called: and whom he called, them he also justified: and whom he justified, them he also glorified* (Romans 8:29-30).

There is much more to the purpose of God than you sometimes understand. God's purpose for your life is an intentional, thoughtful, and result-oriented design which, when manifested, will lift you to a new state and glorify Him who created you. When you accept God's dream-plan for your life, you allow the power of an infinite God, who has been working on your success and blessing, to be released unto you.

When you tell Him "Yes," the possibilities for your life will sometimes stagger you, defying all that is known in the natural realm. The process of bringing God's dream for your life to pass is quite an undertaking. God's purpose for you does not happen overnight. It is determined, intentional, creative and conclusive. Compared to His purpose for you, there is no better suggestion as to what you should do with your life. Compared to His will for you, there is no other idea imaginable that can equal His thought. He who placed order in the universe and sustains it in existence can direct your life successfully and bring it to its intended completion.

His purpose for your life is not haphazard or something determined by chance. Your reasons for being here on earth are to fear God, obey His commandments and fulfill the dream He has placed in your heart. You are *born to dream*.

There are many stages in the development of your dream that you need to understand in order to pursue it. The first stage is *choosing*. We are chosen to be in Him before the foundation of the world (Ephesians 1:4). At that moment, His divine purpose was defined. He already knows the end from the beginning. He goes back through eternity to bring humanity to the point in time where each member of the human race is capable of fulfilling His will, should each so choose. Since creation, God's will for all of mankind is that none should perish, but that all should have everlasting life (John 3:16).

The second stage is *foreknowledge*. In the kingdom of heaven, your spirit is matched with God's purpose. He is the "Father of all spirits" (Hebrews 12:9). At this point, God already knows what type person you will be on earth. His foreknowledge allows Him to make the determination for your best use. While He gives you the privilege of choosing His will (you are a free moral agent), His plan will bring you the ultimate fulfillment in life. When His Word came to Jeremiah in Jeremiah 1:5,

"Before I formed thee in the belly, I knew thee," God was telling Jeremiah the best decision he could make was to accept His will. Jeremiah's excuse of youth was insignificant. God had already prepared for His purpose to be fulfilled in Jeremiah from the beginning. His statement about his limitations was a moot point.

Stage three is *predestination,* the eternal stamping of God's purpose for your life. When God said in Jeremiah 1:5, *"Before thou camest forth out of the womb I sanctified thee,"* God set Jeremiah aside for a specific mission. He was stamped for *greatness!*

His specific plan for your life was sealed prior to your birth. You are set aside for the fulfillment of His divine purpose. Many times it is because of the prayers of your fore-parents that the blessing of God rests upon you. It is because of God's promise to them that God has laid His hand upon you. As God said to Abraham, *"And in thy seed shall all the nations of the earth be blessed; because thou hast obeyed My voice"* (Genesis 22:18). Hannah's vow unto the Lord when she was barren predestined (stamped) her son Samuel for *greatness* (I Samuel 1:11).

Stage four is our *calling*—the revelation of God's predetermined plan for your life. This is the time when you have the option of responding in obedience or not. Many do not respond favorably to their predetermined purpose in life because they have not been exposed to the beauty of allowing God's will to be preeminent in their experience. On the other hand, others have been around the Church all of their lives and want to exert their own will above the will of God.

God gets the attention of those He has predestined for

greatness in different ways. He uses: 1) visual experiences, as in the burning bush miracle for Moses; 2) a still small voice, as He did with Samuel; 3) visions of seraphim and cherubim, as in Isaiah and Ezekiel; and 4) a normal speaking voice, as with Jeremiah.

Don't make the mistake, however, of thinking that you can keep on running and that someday God will bring a whale for you, as He did with Jonah. Depending on the magnitude of your purpose, many times God will go and find somebody else to fulfill your predestination when you are unwilling. One of the greatest ministers of this century, Kathryn Kuhlman, always believed that two other men were called to the ministry she had received, but they refused to accept God's calling for them.

After responding favorably to the call of God, even Moses was denied the opportunity to go into the land of Canaan—a land into which God had predestined him to lead His people. Don't take your chances and wait until you're ready to accept! He might not wait around for you to decide if His choice for your life is right for you. He has the best in mind for us; He, as our Creator, *knows* what will make us *most* happy. When we recognize it, we need to accept His calling.

Stage five is *justification*. This is the part of the dream where God deals with your feelings of inadequacy. He tells you "Say not" that: 1) like Abraham, you are too old; 2) like Moses, you can't talk; 3) with Isaiah, you have unclean lips; 4) as Deborah, you are a woman; 5) just like Jeremiah, you are too young; 6) like Peter, you already know Him; or 7) just as Paul, you have a thorn in the flesh. God's plan has already accounted for your inadequacies, and He has given you the right and power to do for Him what He wants done.

In Romans 5:1-2, the Word says that we are justified by faith to accomplish the dream that God has predestined for us to accomplish. God does not call you because of what you can do for Him, He calls you because of what He wants to do *in you* and *for you*. The fulfillment of your God-given dream is not based on your own goodness; it is based on God's purpose. Some say to me that I am a "good preacher"—whatever that is. To those I graciously respond (remembering certainly that it is by His grace) that if they have been helped by anything I have said, then to God be the glory. However, I strongly urge them to be aware that "I don't preach because *I am good;* I preach because *He is God.*"

> *I am crucified with Christ: nevertheless I live; yet not I, but Christ liveth in me:* and the life which I now live, I live by the faith of the Son of God, *who loved me and gave himself for me* (Galatians 2:20, emphasis added).

Stage six represents our *glorification*. At this stage, it is time for us to shine in the fulfillment of our dreams. Now that we know who we are, and we are not ashamed of being just that, God can move in us and bring to pass the dream He has instilled inside us. Your God-given gifts will be manifested, and they will bring you prosperity even at times when others are not prospering. This evident blessing "in season and out of season" will establish God as the primary doer or cause of blessing in the minds of those around you and so establish you as one whom the Lord has laid His hand upon in favor.

Sometimes people, who are in the same boat as you are, view you as being just like they are. Some cannot recognize that God has put something special in you because you are no further advanced in life than they. In Genesis 40, which relates the experience of Joseph with the baker and the butler, the butler did not recognize the blessing of God upon Joseph's life. They all prospered because of Joseph, but did not praise God for what He was doing for them through Joseph.

Joseph seized the opportunity of using his gift to promote his cause to the butler. Sometimes we try to give out our resumé of spiritual qualifications, which we feel can help God use us to His glory. But if you try to exalt yourself, you will be abased. Instead, if you humble yourself, He will exalt you in due time (I Peter 5:6). Yes, you must wisely promote what God has given you, but remember that the ". . . heart of the king is in the hand of the Lord. . ." (Proverbs 21:1). God will turn the heart of the king to your benefit when it is time. As David sang in the Psalms concerning the life of Joseph,

> *He sent a man before them, even Joseph, who was sold for a servant: Whose feet they hurt with fetters: he was laid in iron: Until the time that his word came: the Word of the Lord tried him* (Psalms 105:17-19).

Joseph remained in prison another two years after interpreting the dreams of the baker and the butler. Although telling the butler to remember him when he was restored to his post (Genesis 40:14-15), the butler forgot (Genesis 40:23). That is the nature of man—to forget the kindness that he has been shown. Being used and forgotten is part of the price you pay for being a dreamer. However, the Lord is not forgetful, and He will bring you out of prison after you have shown that you can hold onto His promise. You will ". . . reap in due season if you faint not" (Galatians 6:9). Though you are in prison, always remember: you were *born to dream!*

# Chapter Six
# **Your Dream Will Take You to the Top**

*And Pharaoh said unto his servants, Can we find* such a one *as this* is, *a man in whom the Spirit of God* is? (Genesis 41:38).

In Genesis 41, Joseph successfully interprets Pharoah's dreams and is made second in command in the land of Egypt. The Spirit manifested Himself so powerfully in Joseph that no one could deny the divine source of his wisdom, but had to follow his inspiration in order to save the country and surrounding nations during the years of famine that plagued the earth (Genesis 41:56-57).

From this dramatic narrative, we learn that the principal and primary purpose of God's anointing in our lives is to help others come into the knowledge of Jesus' saving power. The anointing—the power of the Holy Ghost—empowers us to be witnesses of the saving grace of Jesus.

Of course, the power of the Holy Ghost also gives us the personal empowerment to live for the Lord and to follow His commandments. Prior to being anointed, our function in the Body of Christ is to learn the ways of God and to share our testimonies. This is our period of preparation and observation. During the beginning stages of our walk with God, those who are put in spiritual authority over us will observe the Lord's purpose and intention for our lives. It is during this time that the Lord speaks to His shepherds and teachers, moving them to prepare us and direct us in the way that will bring the fulfillment of the dream and will of God for our lives. During this time, God will teach us and take us through many circumstances to get us ready for "our day."

With the anointing, God strengthens and enables us so that we are ready to perform. When God manifests Himself inside us with His mighty, gentle presence, nothing will be able to hold us back. The Holy Spirit will prepare both the way and the means for us to be a blessing to others.

Just as He was with Joseph, God will be with us through the entire journey of our lives, whether the road leads us into pits, prisons, etc. God watches over His dream and purpose for our lives. In His time, when He is ready, He will call upon that which He has placed within us; when He manifests it, nothing will hold us back.

Sometimes we feel that we are ready to "go forth" before the Lord's time. At these times, we may become unresponsive to the spiritual leadership God has placed in our lives. We cannot become so consumed with our own purpose and how we feel the Lord is leading us that we become lackadaisical in the things that we have been assigned to do in our church or ministry. In our excitement at finding out what God has in mind for us, we may begin to feel that the fulfillment of our dreams is most important and neglect the things that deserve our full attention at the moment. God will give us the time to develop what He has stirred up in us. He had to get us started. Now he has to harness our energy to accomplish our dream in His perfect timing, so that everyone whom it was meant to reach can be blessed by it.

*Though he were a Son, yet learned he obedience by the things which he suffered; and being made perfect, he became the  author of eternal salvation unto all that obey him* (Hebrews 5:8-9).

One important quality about Joseph that we can all benefit from hearing about is his faithfulness at every level of his dream development. Whether he was enslaved or in prison, he worked diligently on whatever was put before him. His duties were given to him and supervised by another man, under whose authority he was obedient, before he could be entrusted with responsibilities of his own. His faithfulness to God no matter where he was or what he was doing enabled God to bless him so that he flourished anywhere—as a coordinator in a prison, a manager of a house or ruler of a kingdom. Doing the will of God gave him the most pleasure; one could say that he developed a holy indifference to his circumstances. To be sure, he must have had to fight the repugnance we feel when we encounter undesirable personalities and dis-agreeable living conditions, but he rose above all of them. He didn't let it make him ugly; instead, he transformed them by the grace of God manifested in his life.

The outstanding quality of his character was what caused great men to trust him with their wealth. He was consistent in his fidelity. Too many times, we have not practiced the principle of faithfulness. This principle requires us to "be faithful with that which is another man's" before God will "give us our own." Before God will commit to our trust the "true riches which are in Christ" (Luke 16:11), He will try us to see if we can be dependable with someone else's blessing. If we cannot be trusted, we are not ready to be brought forth in authority—spiritual or natural. If we can keep others' trust, then we are ready to move up into the next realm of spiritual responsibility. We may not necessarily be called to go out into our own ministry, under our own name. In the vision of God, there is room for the fulfillment of the parts we are to play (our dream) within the greater vision of the ministry right where we are. When we have proven ourselves faithful, God will give us more responsibility in the vision that He has established.

Some will find it necessary to get up and go to the place that the Lord shall show them. If our plans are from the Lord, those who are spiritual will discern and confirm God's direction for our lives. We shouldn't look for allies and supporters of our desires; we are to look for the blessed will of God as He speaks from the mouth of those who are known for giving sound doctrine and spiritual advisement. If it is His will, then our dream is "safe in His arms." If it is not, we might be in store for the ride of our lives inside the "belly of a whale"; or worse yet, like Moses, we may never be permitted to enter the Promised Land that we were predestined to lead others into.

Choices regarding our calling are critical, and we cannot afford any mistakes. How we respond to our callings affects the direction of our lives. We need to seek God and know exactly what His will is for us. It is time to choose, time to set our feet onto solid ground. We should ask God if we are to go left, go right, or if we are on the right track. We know that each time we are mistaken with regard to something as important as our calling, it takes much time and energy to get back to where we need to be. We're not happy until we are in the center of His will. We feel most fulfilled when we are where He wants us. When we find what we are looking for, we find that we wouldn't want it any other way. So let's ask the Lord to help us to see His will clearly, so that we don't miss it.

The development of our gifts takes time and may occur in different stages of development. Some have a gift, but it is not yet time for it to be manifested. Others have a gift, and it is being manifested. Still others claim to be endowed with a particular gift, but do not really have a gift in that area at all; their gift might be in a totally different area, one they have not explored or discovered yet. Let God define His purpose in us. Boasting in a gift that we do not have is like having clouds and wind without rain (Proverbs 25:14).

Our spiritual gifts will mature through various stages. The first stage is the "seed." At this initial stage, we have a gift, but it is not ready to bear fruit. It is usually at this time that we are unable to recognize what God has placed within us, but others with sharper spiritual sense (and distance enough to be objective about us) take note and lead us so that we can be developed.

The second stage of growth is the "sprout." Our gifts become recognizable at this point in our development. We have begun to use our gifts under close spiritual supervision. We are also beginning to recognize God's divine purpose as He manifests Himself through us. During the sprout stage, most of us try to duplicate what we have seen other, more developed, vessels do. Emulating good role models is all right for now, as we are sprouts that do not know where our eventual development will bring us. Sprouts also look alike: young and tender, and without the definable characteristics of more mature plants.

The third stage in gift development is the "plant" or "sapling stage." Our gift is now evident, and we are using that gift to help strengthen others. There is a certainty in knowing what God's purpose is for our lives. We recognize what He has and has not gifted us for, and we are going about doing the thing He has told us to do. We are giving life to others.

The fourth stage in gift development is the "tree." We become established, manifesting gifts that will benefit many. What differentiates the tree from the sapling is that not only do we help others, we are developing little saplings or seedlings of our own, which will grow to be mature as well. The depth of our roots and strength of our limbs support others in various stages of development; our fruitfulness helps to prepare others with the same gift. We shouldn't be fooled into trying to manifest prematurely to those who are so thirsty that they take up all that we have. If our roots are not deep enough, we will eventually dry out from the burden that others will place upon us. If we have God-given gifts, our talents will "make room for us and bring us before great men." However, it takes more than just a gift to keep us in the place of greatness. We must have some depth of our roots.

We ought to remember this principle as we allow the Lord to build His divine work in us: the higher the tree, the deeper the roots; the taller the building, the lower the foundation. Our height will only be in proportion to our depth. In Genesis 41:16, Joseph was ready to be elevated. When he was 17, he boastfully resounded his dreams to his brethren and parents. While his father Jacob should have embraced this young dreamer, Joseph also had a lot to learn about how to carry himself as an anointed vessel of the Lord. Sometimes it is not that we are not gifted, but that we carry ourselves in an arrogant manner that is abrasive to those around us. Our proud spirit runs people away and keeps them from supporting us in the very thing that God has certainly put within us to bless them. That is why teaching is important: we must learn to carry ourselves in *humility*—as in the fear of the Lord and in respect for those around you. Even the little children are worthy of all respect, because each person is important to God, and we never know who is carrying the divine anointing of God. Joseph learned humility through suffering. From being thrown in a pit, enslavement, and imprisonment for something he did not do, a spiritual portal of opportunity was opened up for Joseph by which he was readied to be lifted up to his predestined status, so that his God-given dreams and gifts might be manifested for all to benefit.

The chronology of his spiritual maturing is certainly worthy of examination for comparison with our own lives. At age 17, Joseph declares: *"I have dreamed a dream"* (Genesis 37:9). From there, he was thrown into the pit, then sold into slavery, then went to prison. At age 28, he told the butler and baker, *"Do not interpretations belong to God? Tell me them, I pray you"* (Genesis 40:8). Afterward, he sent out his spiritual resumé to try to leverage himself out of his situation, but ended up staying in prison for two more years. At age 30, after being humbled through his suffering, he declared: *"It is not in me. God shall give Pharaoh an answer of peace"* (Genesis 41:16). His submission to God's sovereign power is evident in his spirit. He comes across as certain and not arrogant, confident and not cocky. His mature answer to Pharaoh signaled that he was ready to go to the top. His suffering for something he did not do (just as Christ would suffer in innocence) has taught him obedience and humility. Now free from pride and vengeance, there was nothing to hold him down anymore. It was time for him to rise to the top.

## Chapter Seven
# Take Me to My Dreamer

*And Joseph* was *the governor over the land, and he* it was *that sold to all the people of the land: and Joseph's brethren came and bowed down themselves before him* with *their faces to the earth* (Genesis 42:6).

In Genesis 42:1-38, Jacob sent his sons to buy corn in Egypt, signaling the beginning of the provision God had for them. God had set it up well ahead of time by bringing Joseph to Egypt before the rest. He gave Joseph time to get in the right position to help his people, especially his own family, teaching them all valuable lessons in the process.

God's plan for His people is complete. When we collectively follow His purpose, we all benefit from the results. Each person is important in the design of God. Each member can positively affect the whole Body of Christ with his or her unique gifts; each gift that God has invested in His people is important to all of us.

We should always try to build others up with all of our ability. But we recognize that there are those times when we do not contribute to love, fellowship and unity.

When we fail to build up the Body of Christ, other people are definitely affected. When we allow envy to separate us from our brothers and sisters, we will pay a price. No, it may not come as something that is actively working against us, but there will be something that we will be lacking that the person we were envious toward would have fulfilled in us. The Church is the one place where people of all walks of life and experiences can come and blend into the purpose of God through salvation. It is God's intention for each joint to supply that which is necessary for the benefit of the entire Body (Ephesians 4:16).

If they can't come to the Church to get what they need, *where else can they go?* This design of God, that we come to Him with and through each other as the people He has redeemed, makes it expedient for us to accept and allow God to move in and use each member of His Body as He sees fit. As the Holy Spirit gives gifts as He pleases, who are we to not accept the ones He has anointed and gifted to serve us? Many times, because of our perceptions of others who come from different backgrounds or those we know well but who have made mistakes in their lives, we shut out, shun and isolate the very ones who, when our hard times come, can bring us the help that we need.

Each vessel that God has raised up has been strategically placed as determined by His divine foreknowledge and predestination. The saying, "Father knows best," is most certainly the case with our heavenly Father, who has charted our course of success from the foundation of the world. It is a sad dialogue when we hear of churches and saints discarding those they did not think worthy of the blessed grace, goodness and mercy of the same God whom they say was merciful to them. The Apostle Paul admonishes us in this way in Romans 2:1-4:

*Therefore thou art inexcusable, O man, whosoever thou art that judgest: for wherein thou judgest another, thou condemnest thyself; for thou that judgest doest the same things. But we are sure that the judgment of God is according to truth against them which commit such things. And thinkest thou this, O man, that judgest them which do such things, and doest the same, that thou shall escape the judgment of God? Or despisest thou the riches of His goodness and forbearance and longsuffering; not knowing that the goodness of God leadeth thee to repentance?*

It is a further testimony of the grace of God when those who have been thrown away by self-righteous saints go on to realize the God-given dream for their lives. God provides for them in other ways, with other vessels. It is a shame when God's people cannot look to each other—and to their own people first of all—for their deliverance. We may unknowingly throw away the ones that we need—those who can really bless us—because of how we treat each other at times.

It is even more regrettable when the anointed children of God find the need to look and see the prosperity in the lives of those who don't profess to know God. Something is terribly wrong when we have to look to Egypt (the symbol of the heathen world) for life, for fear that where the Lord told us to be cannot sustain us.

In Genesis 42, we see the power of keeping designated people in our life. Joseph's dream came to pass 22 years after he told his brothers and parents about it. The corn sheaves of his brothers and father would bow down to his sheaf. The symbol of provision—feeding—comes to pass miraculously, just as the Lord had inspired Joseph. He knew that one day he would be the principle provider for his entire family.

His brothers bowed down to him just as the Lord had shown him, and Joseph recognized his brethren when they came to him. This is one of the important character qualities we must maintain even if we have been envied and despised for our dreams: we must remember who our brothers are—even if they forget us. Joseph uses his position for good, to teach them how to appreciate the gift they had rejected.

In Genesis 42:17, we see Joseph giving his brothers a taste of the experience that their envy had inflicted upon him. Though he didn't give them the true prison experience he had gone through, he did detain them to allow them to feel what it was like to be controlled by someone else. Instead of satisfying a burning desire for revenge, which some would have gratified in similar circumstances, Joseph allowed the Holy Ghost to show him how to teach his brothers a lesson in a less severe manner. Although tempted, God had been so good to Joseph that he just couldn't inflict such pain upon his brothers. His love for his brothers overwhelmed his past hurts, and his love for God, who had always forgiven him, caused him to extend the same mercy to his brothers.

We know we have forgiven others when the love we carry in our hearts won't allow us to get back at those who have hurt us. Yes, we remember the incidents, but we are powerless to be bitter, for we are full of God's *love*. Listening to his brothers, Joseph understood their conversation and notes that, although 22 years have passed since his brothers threw him into the pit, their remorse remained with them. What a spiritual strain to carry such remorse for 22 years, *not knowing* that there is mercy to forgive them for the wrong they have done. Times like these are the God-given moments when those of us who have been done wrong have a tremendous opportunity to *restore* those who have wronged us. Galatians 6:1 helps us to understand the power of restoring those who have been wrong:

> *Brethren, if a man be overtaken in a fault, ye which are spiritual, restore such an one in the spirit of meekness; considering thyself, lest thou also be tempted.*

Joseph used the lesson of "sinless condemnation" to help his brothers understand the experience. This lesson humbles us, showing us how to be used by God even when we are judged wrongly for something that we did not do. This is the experience of our Lord Jesus, who was jailed, badgered, mocked and crucified for something that He did not do. The lesson of bearing wrongs patiently helps strengthen our character and temper our spirits to be sensitive to the cries of mankind. Like Jesus, we have the opportunity to say *". . . forgive them, for they know not what they do"* (Luke 23:34).

Jacob also lived under the burden of his past mistakes. He recognized that he had the power to diffuse his sons' envy against their brother, Joseph. Twenty-two years earlier, when Joseph's dream was mentioned, Jacob should have readily spotted that the gift of dreams had shown up in one of his sons. After all, this was his own gift and the gift evident in the life of his father Isaac and his grandfather, Abraham. When it showed up in Joseph, he should have protected him and helped to nurture the anointing in his life.

Now, more than ever, we need to protect our "Josephs" and "Josephines"—those God has anointed with great vision and insight. We need "Jacobs"—those with the wisdom of God—to nurture and prepare God's next anointed army of spiritual warriors. We also need our Josephs in place, so that when adversity comes, their gifting and anointing will be on hand to bring us through. Their supply will be there when we need it.

Jacob was rendered powerless to make a decision that would benefit the entire family because of his loss in the past. Sometimes our past hurts and disappointments will keep us from moving on when another opportunity arrives from which we can benefit. We reject help, and even love, because we are so hurt that we feel suspicious and untrusting. As a result, God's Holy Spirit is not allowed to flow freely in us as He once did. So when our pain outweighs His power, our sorrow outweighs His satisfaction, our brokenness outweighs His blessedness, our

despair outweighs His deliverance, our uncertainty outweighs His understanding, and our poverty outweighs His
prosperity, we can call on Him. He will answer us with
the dreamer who can show us how to turn pain into
power, sorrow into satisfaction, brokenness into blessedness, despair into deliverance, uncertainty into understanding, and poverty into prosperity. *Lord, take me to my
dreamer!*

## Chapter Eight
# Believing in My Dreamer

*And they answered, Thy servant our father is in*
*good health, he is yet alive. And they bowed down*
*their heads, and made obeisance* (Genesis 43:28).

In Genesis 43:1-34, when his family was again without food, Joseph has his brothers bring Benjamin with
them in order for them to be allowed to see him.
Sometimes the Lord will allow times of drought to come
upon us in our walk with Him. These times teach us valuable lessons about trust and faith in what He is able to do,
and has said He would do for us. Sometimes this is just
what it takes for us to come to the point where we recognize our total need and dependence on Him to provide for
our every need. It is a point of revelation and realization
that all our help comes from the Lord (Psalms 121:1-2) so
that you must therefore, in the words of a famous chorus,
". . . Praise God from whom all blessings flow."

God orchestrates situations and circumstances that will
serve to bring us to this point of confessing Him as our
source. Many times our own decisions provide the back-
drop from which His lessons are learned. We get ourselves
into situations that He has to get us out of because we did

not first ask for His direction. He is faithful to deliver us when we cry unto Him: He sends us His Word of instruction to get us out of our self-inflicted circumstances.

> *. . . then they cried unto the Lord in their trouble and he saveth them out of their distresses. He sent His Word, and healed them, and delivered them from their destructions* (Psalm 107:19-20).

When God sends His Word of healing and deliverance to us, He does so through someone else—not just anyone, but an anointed vessel—a dreamer. It is important for us to understand that we must believe the Word, and we need to obey the messenger or dreamer in order for us to access whatever God sends us. God has decided for us to be blessed by using people whom He chooses, predestines, calls and anoints to bring us His blessing. Men and women who are equipped by the Holy Ghost with special gifts can place within our hands the miracle that we are looking for. When He speaks His Word through them, we can be healed and delivered from our situations.

God is a good Father. He pulls us out of the circumstance we have created for ourselves. He wants us to understand what He has done for us and why, so that we may move to a new level. He wants us to come out with some insight into what caused our drought or bondage and what it is going to take for us to stay delivered. He does not want us to go back to our old way of living and decision-making that got us into the mess in the first place. This is why He said to the woman caught in adultery, whom He delivered from the stoning crowd, *". . . go and sin no more"* (John 8:11). The lesson that woman gained from her experience and the words of deliverance taught her how to walk in faith, not allowing the enemy of her soul to bind her again.

When Jesus sends our deliverance it is always with a Word. It can come through preaching, teaching, or exhorting; it can come through a song, poem or story; it can come through a man, woman, child or even a donkey. It is always through His speaking that we are healed and delivered. That Word, when mixed with faith, has the power to change the circumstances of our lives. That Word will also remind us of what it took for us to be healed and delivered. That Word will be our reference point upon which we build our faith, to "go on and sin no more." That Word is also our lesson, which will help us to grow beyond our present boundaries (limitations) and bondages (hindrances).

In the text of Genesis 43, the scene shifts back to Canaan, where the provisions that Jacob's sons have purchased in Egypt have now been consumed. Often it seems that as long as we are doing fine, eating everything we can get our hands on, we don't perceive the need to progress further in life. Although we know that there is a greater blessing that we need in another place, we will sit where we are until we have eaten up everything there is to eat, before realizing that we need to get up and go to more fertile ground. Sometimes we'd rather starve than humble ourselves and go to the place where we know we can be fed, where we know we can get what we need. Other times, when we *do* go, we only want to buy just enough to feed us for a little while—enough to last us for a few weeks or months. God wants our whole attention and our whole hearts. He wants to give us the food that will satisfy us always—Himself (John 6:50).

The man who found the field wherein was a great treasure sold everything he had just to buy that field (Matthew 13:44). The man who found the pearl of great price sold everything he had, just to obtain the greatest treasure he could own (Matthew 13:46). We must learn to count as worthy the place where the blessing flows forth to feed us and water us with His goodness. We must count worthy the one whom God sends to feed us and to give us water when we are hungry and thirsty.

Judah, starving because of his envy (Judah recommended that Joseph be sold into slavery in Genesis 37:26), pleads with his father to allow them to take their younger brother to Egypt so that they may obtain food. Again, as he had done 22 years earlier, Judah was not really as concerned about his brother as much as he was concerned about his own situation. Back then, he was more concerned about the profit that could be gained from the sale of his brother than the very life of his brother. Now, when he is hungry, he is again more concerned about himself than his own brother, but decides to seek his help. In his hunger, he makes a commitment to "be his brother's keeper." This willingness is what God wanted to hear. God wants to instill in our hearts the commitment to look out for someone else.

Jacob yields to the need of his family. He acknowledges that everything is now in the hands of God. This point of surrender is what God wants us to reach. Now "the ball is in our court." When we are not "all booked up"—busied with circumstances, occupied by responsibilities or filled up with self-love—but have made a room for Him, then He can enter. Our availability opens a place where God can send our word of healing and deliverance. Our openness takes the brakes off of what He wants to do in our lives. When God sees that we have met His criteria, that we moved out in faith with whatever we have, He will prepare the house for us to be blessed.

When Joseph saw that his brothers were obedient to his commandment, he prepared a place for them to eat in his own house. Sometimes, like Joseph's brethren, the imminent blessing seems almost too good to be true. We know within our hearts that we have been "wronger than two left shoes"; but regardless of our unworthiness and propensity to make mistakes, God shows us He is spreading a table for us to sit down and feast in His presence. That incomprehensible love is what blows our mind about God. We know that He knows everything about us, right and wrong, yet He still wants to bless us in spite of ourselves.

When we know we have been wrong, we should *bring a present!* No, it won't necessarily make up for what we have done, but the gesture shows that we have acknowledged our mistakes.

Sometimes when God begins to deal with us, He begins with a few light conversations, just to get us to the point to be ready to open up to Him. If God were to tell us all about ourselves at one time, we would be so discouraged that we would give up on ever trying to serve Him. Thankfully, He does not show us all of ourselves the first day, but reveals Himself to us, and ourselves to us, a little at a time.

At seeing Benjamin, Joseph's heart was so full of the love that God had poured into him, he could not refrain himself and had to run out of the room to compose himself (Genesis 43:30). Although he may have wanted to be bitter and revengeful, God had been so good to him that he wanted to share this goodness with his brothers. This meeting was a test for him as well, to know that he had overcome the bitterness and anger from what his brothers had done to him.

God will prepare everything He wants for us to eat, and He will set us up in His house in a manner that will cause us to marvel. He will tell His dreamer (messenger) what is going on inside our house, our family and our conversations with friends. Our anointed dreamer will minister to us in ways that will astonish us. We ought to glorify God when He sets us at His table. He is close at hand. When He is that near to us, our blessings of healing and deliverance are right in front of us. Eat and be merry in the house of God. The joy of the Lord is our strength. *I cried to the Lord, and He heard me and sent me a prophetic dreamer!* If we believe, God is showing us He *will* establish and prosper us:

> *And they rose early in the morning, and went forth into the wilderness of Tekoa: and as they went forth, Jehoshaphat stood and said, Hear me, O Judah, and ye inhabitants of Jerusalem; Believe in the LORD our God, so shall ye be established; believe his prophets, so shall ye prosper* (II Chronicles 20:20).

## Chapter Nine
# Recognizing My Dreamer

*And Judah said, What shall we say unto my lord? what shall we speak or how shall we clear ourselves? God hath found out the iniquity of thy servants: behold, we are my lord's servants, both we, and he also with whom the cup is found* (Genesis 44:16).

In Genesis 44:1-34, before his brothers went back to their father, Joseph put his silver cup in Benjamin's sack, so that he could keep him as his servant, teaching his brothers another important lesson. There is so much that the Lord wants to do in us. If we only knew what the Lord has prepared for those He loves, it would be impossible for us to take it all in. As we have seen, *we* are the first and biggest obstacle we must overcome in order to acknowledge and move forward in the gifting that God has promised us.

To help us understand His will and blessing for our life, God sends an anointed vessel or dreamer to show us the desire of God for our lives. Whether pastor, evangelist, prophet, teacher—man, woman or child—God's messenger will help to bring us into the predestination for our lives. This is the way that He operates.

Oftentimes we are not able to recognize those whom God has sent to make a difference in our lives and give us spiritual insight into His will and purpose. This oversight can inhibit our understanding of the full purpose of God for us. However, God is a master communicator, and He will cause us to understand what He wants through some other means—through many diverse experiences, if necessary.

Frequently we listen to, but do not internalize, the messages spoken by the vessels He is using, because: 1) they look like us, or are from the same race or nationality; 2) they are from our community, and so we think we know them; 3) they share the same background, which makes us feel they are not qualified to know any more than we do; or 4) they are too close to us as friends or relatives, and so our closeness keeps us from hearing God in their words. These and other reasons keep us from accessing the great grace and anointing that accompanies the messengers God sends to us. That is why the servants of the Lord can't often allow us to get close. They know that if we see their humanity, we will have difficulty seeing their divine anointing.

Not everyone can see God in anyone. If God is to deliver us (especially African-Americans), He is going to use someone who looks just like us. He sent Moses to his own people, Esther to her own people, and Martin Luther King to his own people. God is not prejudiced, for He is no respecter of persons; but He knows that a familiar face and voice will give us a sense of honor and dignity, that one of our own is being used mightily by the Lord to bring blessings to us. God told Moses that there would come a time when His people would ask for a king. Therefore, God instructed Moses to tell the people that when they did so, the king was to be one of their own brethren (Deuteronomy 17:15). What better testimony than for God to raise up someone from our midst in which to manifest His power? What better testimony than for God to raise up someone from the "hood," the "barrio," the "country," et cetera?

He gives us wonderful opportunities, but all too often we cannot recognize our dreamer. Peter did not recognize his dreamer, Jesus, who walked by the disciples on the water while they were in a ship in the middle of a storm. Peter said to Jesus, "If it is you, bid me come" (Matthew 14:28). Peter then walked on the water with Jesus.

The two Emmaus travelers walking home from Jerusalem after the death and resurrection of the Lord did not recognize Jesus, who rebuked them and then taught them with authority out of the Scriptures (Luke 24:13-27). It was not until He was at the table in their house, breaking bread, that they did recognize Him, at which time He vanished (Luke 24:30-31).

In Genesis 44, Joseph targets the youngest son, Benjamin, to test his brethren. Benjamin, who was Joseph's brother by the same mother, Rachel, was a favorite of his father Jacob. Joseph sets up almost the same scenario of 22 years ago to try these men, to see if they had strong commitment to their younger brother, and most of all, to their father who loved him. In the past, they failed this test miserably; Joseph uses this situation to see if they have changed.

Coming face to face with their dreamer, they still did

not recognize him. He had sat them around the table in order of their birth and gave more food to his younger brother—surely they would have begun to get the hint that he could be their brother. Uncertainty over our past will blind us to the present possibility of God. When we have unconfessed sin in our lives, it will make us uncertain of the future; we will not know when retribution for our wrong is going to come upon us. Unforgiveness blinds us to the wonderful possibilities that God has for us. It also keeps us from seeing the miraculous, the supernatural and the anointing. That is why we must first confess our sins, so that we may enter into the realm of the possible for our lives. Unconfessed sin can cause us to place limits on what we believe can happen for us.

Judah, the lawgiver, must be the one to stand up for Benjamin. He had not done so for Joseph 22 years earlier. His desire to profit from the disadvantage of his younger brother had come back to haunt him many times. God had dealt with his unrighteousness in Genesis 38 in the matter of his daughter-in-law, Tamar. She had been promised in marriage to the third son of Judah after her previous two husbands (Judah's first two sons) had died. Judah promised her the younger son, as was the custom of the land, but had not delivered him to her when he was of age. When Judah went to shear his sheep in Timnath, she disguised herself as a harlot and met him in the city. For her services, Judah gave her his signet ring and bracelet as a deposit, until he could bring her the full payment of a lamb. When he sent his servant to bring her the payment, she had returned home and could not be found. Some months later, when it was discovered she was pregnant,

Judah was among the leaders who insisted that she should be stoned for her folly. When she showed him his signet and bracelet (articles he had pledged to her for her services), he declared that she has been more righteous than he was in his dealings. This lesson of righteous treatment is Judah's tempering experience. It is through this experience that he is taught fairness. Judah's plea to Joseph for his younger brother, Benjamin, on behalf of his brothers was a sign that he was ready to be blessed. His concern, first of all for his brother and then for his father, is evident when he asks Joseph to take him instead of Benjamin. This offering of self in the place of another is the love for our brothers and sisters that God seeks. *"Greater love hath no man than this that a man lay down his life for a friend"* (John 15:13).

If we love selflessly by being our brother's keeper, we will increase our sensitivity to recognize our dreamer when God sends him or her to us, and thus more clearly perceive God's calling on our lives.

## Chapter Ten
# My Dreamer Is Still Alive

*And we know that all things work together for good to them that love God, to them who are the called according to his purpose* (Romans 8:28).

In Genesis 45:1-28, Joseph revealed his identity to his brothers, explained how God had His hand in his being sent to Egypt and sent his brothers home to tell his father that he is still alive. Being reunited with his family must have seemed a dream that had little possibility of coming true. Circumstances had carried him far from those he loved, and he must have wondered if he'd ever see them again.

In some cases where people are separated by distance over long periods of time, they grow apart and have difficulty relating when they do get together or speak to one another. But God works behind the scenes, moving in the hidden places of the heart to restore all things to wholeness. God can work on both separated parties individually, causing them to seek reconciliation for past offenses, even for things done that unknowingly caused bad feelings. The impossible and unthinkable are quite possible for God, who enjoys doing such remarkable things to show His love for us, that we can trust Him, and that much more is to come.

Even when we think we have failed, and there is no hope of getting back what we have lost, God shows us that we are happily mistaken. Sometimes we feel that because we may have passed over or botched up an opportunity, we can't get it back and another one will not come our way. We allow ourselves to live under the shadow of clichés like, "Lightning never strikes twice in the same place," "You never get a second chance," "Strike while the iron is hot," or "It's now or never." These statements can suggest a finality to things and limit our possibilities of action. Even if we have not obtained everything we desired, or have made some mistakes that cost us along the way, there is no reason to count ourselves out of the blessing that God has for us in life.

We must not limit ourselves, for we are the only ones that will do so. God doesn't limit what we can do—we do. He wants to show us that we can obtain all that we are looking for, not just the little part we think we deserve. He says *"Ask and ye shall receive"* (John 16:24) and *"yet ye have not, because ye ask not"* (James 4:2). We ask in proportion to our faith; that is why our faith must be built up. In II Kings 13:16-19, we see this principle in action,

> *And he said to the king of Israel, Put thine hand upon the bow. And he put his hand upon it: and Elisha put his hands upon the king's hands. And he said, Open the window eastward. And he opened it. Then Elisha said, Shoot. And he shot. And he said, The arrow of the LORD's deliverance, and*

*the arrow of deliverance from Syria: for thou shalt
smite the Syrians in Aphek, till thou have consumed them. And he said, Take the arrows. And he
took them. And he said unto the king of Israel,
Smite upon the ground. And he smote thrice, and
stayed. And the man of God was wroth with him,
and said, Thou shouldest have smitten five or six
times; then hadst thou smitten Syria till thou hadst
consumed it: whereas now thou shalt smite Syria
but thrice.*

Yes, there are some times when the window is open
only once for us, such as it was with the young king
Joash, whom Elisha told to smite the ground to have victory over his enemies. He smote the ground three times;
but Elisha, angered with his lack of drive, told Joash that
he should have smitten the ground several times, so that
he could have utterly destroyed his enemy. We limit our
opportunities to receive blessings because we don't know
His grace is there for us, in abundance, to supply all we
need to fulfill simultaneously our dreams and His will.

God's sovereignty, however, can override our own
perceptions and beliefs about what is the extent of the
goodness that shall come to us in our days. He has a way
of bringing things back into their original purpose and
plan even though we have not understood His will,
obeyed His commandment or moved in His time as we
should have. He has a way of bringing His chosen back
together, where they should be. In II Samuel 13 and 14,
we see the story of how God can work a situation for
good and bring those that have been separated back to

their original purpose. After Amnon had raped his half-sister, Tamar, her full brother, Absalom, plotted against him. Two years after the incident, Absalom planned Amnon's death by inviting him along with all of the other king's sons to sheer his sheep. While at the festival, Absalom ordered Amnon to be killed. Afterwards, Absalom went into exile in Geshur for three years.

Although wanting to go to Absalom, King David did not reach out to him. Perceiving that David's heart was moved toward his son, David's general, Joab, used a wise woman to bring a parable to David to encourage him to bring his son back out of his self-imposed exile. In II Samuel 14:14a, the woman instructs David that "Water that is spilled on the ground cannot be gathered up again," meaning that David should get over the loss of Amnon and move forward with his life. She further instructed David about God's intention to bring things back together when she says that God "devises a means that his banished be not expelled from him" (II Samuel 14:14b).

Even in the Church, when at first some have not been agreeable to do the work of God together, God has a way of bringing those He has chosen back together again so that His purpose may be accomplished. The disciple John Mark, the nephew of Barnabas, had left the evangelistic field while on a previous tour with Apostle Paul. When Paul was led to return to those cities, he reminded Barnabas that John Mark left them the previous time. The contention was so strong between them that even they parted company (Acts 15:36-41).

Though this had been the case in this instance, later on in his work, Paul instructed Timothy to bring John

Mark with him, for he was a help to the ministry
(II Timothy 4:11). Sometimes those who are destined to
work together are hindered at first by their immaturity
and human perceptions. Sometimes the one who did not
seem committed to the work in the beginning will have
changed and later become fruitful in the work.

As we examine the text in Genesis 45, Joseph's envious brothers came into direct contact with their dreamer—their gift from God whom they had despised. When
we come face-to-face with an opportunity that we may
have previously ignored, it almost seems unbelievable,
too good to be true! Joseph's brothers were troubled at his
presence because of their memory of what they had done
wrong. Sometimes we are so busy thinking about what
we have done wrong that we will try to deny the wondrous blessing that God is presently bringing into our
lives. It is so beyond what we thought we deserved that
we feel that there must be a "set up" going on somewhere. When God purposes to bless us, it is no set up!
*"The blessing of the Lord maketh rich and addeth no sor-
row with it"* (Proverbs 10:20).

Joseph encouraged his brothers not to be grieved over
their treatment of him so long ago. Joseph was the only
one who had the power to release them from their past. He
was the one who controlled whether they were freed in
their minds or not, for it was against him that they had
sinned. He was the one who could bring everything together by forgiving them and letting them see the greater purpose of God for his life. He released them from the grief
over making a bad decision in the past and encouraged
them to not allow guilt to pound them into nothingness.

Sometimes we are not able to move into the future because of our distaste for ourselves resulting from the decisions we made in the past. We further penalize ourselves with excessive guilt which can manifest itself in many ways. Self-abasement (lowering our self dignity below normal levels), depression and suicide are just some of the expressions that can lead us down a self-destructive path. Always remember: *we are not merely the sum total of our experiences!* Things can change, because God can change *us.* He can bring out the best in us by showing us that we, too, have our own dream to bring into reality, and we should begin to work on it at once. When we find our purpose, we will become quite content to busily work toward positive, constructive, personalized goals.

Joseph helped his brothers to understand the purpose of God in his life and theirs. His dream had been perfected through the human experience of his brothers' envy. *God's sovereignty allows Him to make use of any element of our human experience to accomplish His purpose.* He used the envy of Joseph's brothers to bring to pass the preparation and development of His servant, who would, in turn, minister to those that envied him. Although God did not promote the envy of Joseph's brothers, He did use the outcome of that experience to shape Joseph into the person He desired Him to be.

Many times those who envy us, spread lies about us and hate us, have been used by God to make us prepared vessels who can minister His love, forgiveness and saving power. He is not the source of this persecution, but He will use the experience to teach us a lesson about human nature and His greater divine purpose. One of the ultimate prices we pay for dreaming is that we oftentimes will have to endure rejection. From this experience, we will learn to be patient with those who do not understand the higher principles that we live by. Our ability to overlook or see past others' lack of understanding (which causes prejudice, envy and intolerance) is one of the greatest dimensions of character we can attain. Great men are those whose noble and lofty dreams keep them from being possessed and disturbed by lesser evils.

Relationships that have been healed touch something inside of everyone. Even those who are of differing backgrounds—racial, ethnic, social and otherwise—feel touched when people who have been separated come back together. There is something about reunion that fulfills the deepest desire in all of us. Every human being feels compelled to help facilitate reunions.

When we have paid the price to dream, God will empower us to help those who may have worked against us to get on their feet again. When we get on top, we must not yield to the temptation to taunt or to tease our former detractors about our success, but we must be willing to share with them what we have learned, knowing that our empowerment came from God. When God has taken our lives and orchestrated our deliverance and blessing, like Jacob, we find it is so good that it's almost too good. We will be amazed because all along we have wanted to believe in our dreamer and in their dream, but did not know *how.* When Jacob saw all of the wagons and riches that his son had sent to him, he was revived!

When we see the evidence of God's blessings in our

midst, we too will be revived! That's why we are having revival right now! God's people have seen the evidence in their lives that no matter what has happened in the past, they still have a right to be blessed. His promise to fulfill our dreams has not been revoked and our dreamer is still alive!

## Chapter Eleven
# Dreamers Have Much to Do

*Trust in the LORD with all thine heart; and lean not unto thine own understanding. In all thy ways acknowledge him, and he shall direct thy paths* (Proverbs 3:5-6).

In Genesis 46:1-7,28-34, Joseph is reunited with his father; and in Genesis 47:1-31, Joseph expends all the money and food in Egypt to feed the people in time of famine. In the end, the people willingly become Pharaoh's slaves so as not to starve.

Many of us can look back at our lives and see where we have made decisions before consulting the Lord. Sometimes our decisions were correct, but many times we were without the benefit of God's wisdom, and our decisions brought us limited success, or even pain, frustration and hurt. We must learn to acknowledge Him so that He can direct our paths. Time has a way of teaching us that without the Lord we can do nothing—that is nothing that will bring us any lasting, effective results accompanied by the true joy and peace that we desire. As we continue to grow older, and hopefully wiser, we should begin to understand just how much we don't know and how much we really need the Lord to guide our lives.

Many people ask me, "Reverend, how did you do this?" or "How did you know what to say to that person?" I do not always know, but God leads me to where He wants me to go.

*For as many as are led by the Spirit of God, they are the sons of God* (Romans 8:14).

Romans 8:14 shows us that the leading of the Lord is based upon the Lord, and not upon our disposition. What makes us His is not that we always follow, but that He leads us. It is up to Him to lead us; that is what makes us His children. Sons don't always know where their Father is going; they just follow Him because they like to please Him in all things. Life is a spiritual walk. Even with all that we may know naturally, there are so many things that we don't know about the Spirit that we cannot trust in our own knowledge or "common sense." To follow the Lord, we must trust in Him with all our hearts, not relying only on our own understanding. Christianity is not a way of the mind unaided by faith; it is the way of the Spirit of God. If we are to "know and go," we must be "fed and led" by His Spirit. Following the Spirit is the only way for us to be successful.

Trust *in the LORD, and do good; so shalt thou dwell in the land, and verily thou shalt be fed.* Delight *thyself also in the LORD; and he shall give thee the desires of thine heart.* Commit *thy way unto the LORD; trust also in him; and he shall bring it to pass.* Rest *in the LORD, and wait patiently for him: fret not thyself because of him who prospereth in his way, because of the man who bringeth wicked devices to pass. . . .* Depart *from evil, and do good; and dwell for evermore. . . .* Wait *on the LORD, and keep his way, and he shall exalt thee to inherit the land: when the wicked are cut off, thou shalt see it.* Mark *the perfect man, and behold the upright: for the end of that man is peace* (Psalms 37:3-7,27,34,35, emphasis added*).*

In Psalms 37, the Lord gives the following seven directives to develop ourselves in the way of prosperity: 1) *trust,* or uninhibited confidence and absolute dependence in Him; 2) *delight,* or finding all pleasure in the Lord; 3) *commit,* resolutely submitting all in our hands to God; 4) *rest,* meaning that we should not stress ourselves; He never sleeps, so we should let Him handle our problems; 5) *depart,* or leave off doing evil and the company of those who do; 6) *wait,* holding until further notice; and 7) *mark,* or observe.

To be spiritual, observe those who are. When we learn how to *do* the things they do, we will develop inside of us the environment where God can manifest Himself at any time. Additionally, there are three things which the Scripture admonishes us *not* to do: 1) *fret,* to become anxious and disturbed over something; 2) *anger*, to be frustrated about something or someone; and 3) *wrath*, an action against someone. These things impede the flow of God's Spirit from moving in our lives and from giving us His wisdom and direction. We overcome these impediments by actively *doing* the seven things that the

Scripture says to do. These will lay the groundwork that will make us so *"that ye shall neither be barren nor unfruitful in the knowledge of our Lord Jesus Christ"* (II Peter 1:8).

When God wants to move us from one place to another, He will let us know. We won't have to become anxious about where He wants us to be and what He wants us to do. He *"works in us both to will and to do of His good pleasure"* (Philippians 2:13). We don't have to work in Him; He works in us. In Genesis 46, God makes His will plain to Jacob in the same manner in which he communicated with all of the patriarchs. Before journeying down to Egypt, Jacob needed to hear from the Lord. He began His trip with an historic stop in Beersheba. This is the place he had left when fleeing his brother Esau's wrath after Jacob had stolen his birthright (Genesis 28:10). Beersheba was the blessed land that God had caused him to return to after having been away for 20 years. He was not about to leave this blessed place without a direct Word from the Lord.

Sometimes we move on the first thing that comes to us: a dream, an idea or a voice. But sometimes what caused the dream is what we ate last night. What gave us the idea was our mind, which had been exposed to some carnal knowledge that we transposed into spiritual direction for our life. The voice we heard was the voice of our own desires, which we interpreted to be the voice of God. There are four voices in the world: God's, others', the devil's and ours. We had better be sure that we have heard the right one, or we will experience turmoil and confusion. Jacob wanted to know the mind of the Lord concerning this move. God dealt with him the same way He had dealt with his father, Isaac, his grandfather, Abraham, and his son, Joseph. God spoke to Jacob and told him not to fear to go down into Egypt. God had to tell him this specifically because He originally commanded Isaac not to go into Egypt.

*And the LORD appeared unto him, and said, Go not down into Egypt; dwell in the land which I shall tell thee of: Sojourn in this land, and I will be with thee, and will bless thee; for unto thee, and unto thy seed, I will give all these countries, and I will perform the oath which I swear unto Abraham thy father; And I will make thy seed to multiply as the stars of heaven, and will give unto thy seed all these countries; and in thy seed shall all the nations of the earth be blessed* (Genesis 26:2-4).

In Genesis 46:1-4a, God gave Jacob three specific conditions that would support him in what he was about to do: 1) "I will make you great there"; 2) "I will go with you there"; and 3) "I will bring you back here." In order to build Jacob's confidence that he was indeed hearing God, the Lord told him that Joseph would put his hand upon his eyes (Genesis 46:4b). This reference indicates that when he would die, not only would Joseph be there with him to close his eyes (as someone does when a person expires), but they would all be back in the land of Canaan. This was important to Jacob, for it confirmed to him that Joseph was indeed alive and that his descendants would return to the place where God said He would bless them and multiply them.

When God has something for us to do, there are five characteristics of His will that should be clear to us. If they are not clear, then we need to be more certain that the Lord is, in fact, speaking to us. When God speaks: 1) it is for a definite time; 2) it is for a definite place; 3) it is for a definite purpose; 4) it is for a definite people; and 5) it will yield a definite result. If any one of these characteristics is undefined, then we should seek the Lord to know if the opportunity in front of us is of Him or not. We discern God's will for us also by talking with our spiritual authority—our pastor or others who are known to recognize His voice.

Our instructions need to be just as clear as Jacob's were, because they will affect our lives. After 22 years of separation, Jacob is comforted by the opportunity to see his son, Joseph. "Coming full circle," or reuniting with God's original purpose and plan, is a refreshing experience. For 22 years, Jacob thought his son, born by Rachel—the wife he really loved—to be dead. This revival of his feelings for his long-lost son strengthened Jacob and also brought a sense of completeness to his life that had been missing. This fulfillment brought him satisfaction, since he now saw that God had indeed blessed all of his family in spite of their shortcomings. He then knew for himself the power of God's promise and felt free to die, knowing that everything God said was most certainly true. Jacob was healed in his spirit and had the confidence that he could go to his grave knowing that all of his children would be safe in the arms of God.

When we learn to trust Him, we will not fret over whether He will save our family. We will know that what we have committed to Him, He is able to keep. God had saved (preserved) all of Jacob's sons, and Jacob had lived to see it happen. This should encourage us to know that He will move in our family, too, as we have asked Him to do. Though the time tarries, wait for it, for it will come to pass.

Prior to their arrival in Egypt, Joseph told his family how to talk to Pharaoh. He instructed them to say that they were shepherds, knowing that the Egyptians did not associate with people of this occupation. (Their prejudice against shepherds was a precursor of things to come.)

In Genesis 47, Joseph took his family to Goshen, taking five of his brothers to meet Pharaoh. When they talked with Pharaoh, they asked him to allow them to live in Goshen as Joseph had advised. Because Goshen was the place where cattle, even Egyptian-owned cattle, were sustained, Pharaoh committed this land to the sustenance of the Hebrew family. Joseph had played this situation perfectly, and his brothers, though quiet, now had to realize the kind of power that Joseph wielded in the Egyptian nation (Genesis 45:8).

Joseph brought his father Jacob in to *bless* Pharaoh. No matter what kind of earthly power people may possess, the anointing is the greatest power manifested on the earth. Pharaoh, though the most powerful earthly ruler at that time in history, needed to be blessed by Jacob. Many times we won't witness to people of power and position, because we feel that they are greater than we, when it is just the other way around. Because the hand of God is upon us, that makes us the ones to bless them. People of means and power realize (at least some of them do) that there is a power higher than they are, and that when that power is manifested in the lives of others, they would do well to put themselves in a position to benefit from it.

Pharaoh had enough sense to realize that his entire empire was prospering because of the son of Jacob. Now Pharaoh came face-to-face with the one who raised, trained and blessed the one who was blessing him. What a compliment it was to Jacob to see the glory of his son in Egypt, and realize how God had put him in such a position! What an opportunity it was for Pharaoh to receive such a blessing at the hand of Jacob! When Pharaoh asks him about his life, Jacob tells him his age and shares with him about the misery and pain he has endured. Jacob, though refreshed by the wondrous blessing of seeing his son, is still somewhat plagued by the outcome of his mistakes and by the trials he has been through in his life. At the age of 130, it is harder to let go of failures than it was at 40. Many seniors live in regret because they did not follow wise instructions that were given to them while they were young. It is important for youth to listen to the wisdom that God gives to them through those He has placed in their lives. It will save them a lot of grief and anguish in the future.

Not everyone recovers from the mistakes they made in life. Some made mistakes and now they are insane, sick, diseased, broken, hurt and in pain. We must all learn to trust Jesus and use His Word to guide our lives now. We need to follow the direct leading of the Lord in our youth before age brings additional responsibilities and requirements. Adults need to learn to follow the specific instruction of the Lord. This wisdom will help preserve our lives, and it will be an example to our children that it is a blessing to obey.

Joseph's dream came true; he sustained his entire family. Joseph's dream about the wheat shows the blessing of God's provision in using Joseph to bring food to his brothers. The dream about the sun, moon and 11 stars showed that his family would greatly respect the position of power and responsibility in which God placed Joseph.

After 22 years, the dream came true, and Joseph made use of his power in a way that benefitted those he loved. When God gives us a dream, its outcome should be to benefit those around us. Any dream that is self-gratifying alone is not a dream from God. Our dream is not for us only; it is for those around us. In meeting other's needs, we will find our blessing.

The closing passages of Genesis 47 give us insight into the profound gift of wisdom and administration that God had given Joseph. Joseph literally ran the entire economy. It was his gift that caused the Egyptian nation to be prosperous at a time when other countries were in desolation due to the famine. Jacob and his sons prospered because of Joseph's gift. These were the "best of times." Life was so good that Jacob continued to live for another 17 years. When the blessing comes upon us, it will make us live. In the midst of that goodness, Jacob recognized his mortality and secured a promise from Joseph that when he died he should be buried back home in the land where he was raised.

The blessing of the Lord had enriched Jacob and his entire family. This son who had dared to dream is the reason for the family's great prosperity. Because of the anointing upon Joseph, Jacob charges him with the responsibility of following the commandments of God and the tradition of the family. When we take a stand for what God has said in our lives, others will notice that the anointing is upon our life and will trust us with more than ever before. *"To whom much is given, much is required"* (Luke 12:48). Dreamers have much to do.

## Chapter Twelve
# Dreamers Have Much to Give Up

*Who through faith subdued kingdoms, wrought righteousness, obtained promises, stopped the mouths of lions, quenched the violence of fire, escaped the edge of the sword, out of weakness were made strong, waxed valiant in fight, turned to flight the armies of the aliens. Women received their dead raised to life again: and others were tortured, not accepting deliverance; that they might obtain a better resurrection: And others had trial of cruel mockings and scourgings, yea, more-over of bonds and imprisonment: They were stoned, they were sawn asunder, were tempted, were slain with the sword: they wandered about in sheepskins and goatskins; being destitute, afflicted, tormented; (Of whom the world was not worthy:) they wandered in deserts, and in mountains, and in dens and caves of the earth* (Hebrews 11:1,33-38).

In Genesis 48, Jacob blessed Joseph and his sons before he dies; and in Genesis 49, Jacob spoke prophetically to the rest of his sons, sharing with them a glimpse into their future. We often reflect upon the blessings that have come not only to ourselves, but also to others who have been blessed. We even sit and wonder at the goodness of God in the lives of others. We ask why others seem to get blessed more than we do, because we usually do not know the sacrifices that they have made to see God move in their lives as He does. Fasting, prayer, study, consecration and service are some of the intangibles that we do not always see, and rightly so. In Matthew 6, Jesus tells of the rewards of what "doing in secret" will bring to us openly.

> *And when thou prayest, thou shalt not be as the hypocrites are: for they love to pray standing in the synagogues and in the corners of the streets, that they may be seen of men. Verily I say unto we, They have their reward. But thou, when thou prayest, enter into thy closet, and when thou hast shut thy door, pray to thy Father which is in secret; and thy Father which seeth in secret shall reward thee openly. . . . But thou, when thou fastest, anoint thine head, and wash thy face; That thou appear not unto men to fast, but unto thy Father which is in secret: and thy Father, which seeth in secret, shall reward thee openly* (Matthew 6:4-6,17-18).

In the investment markets, there is an old adage: "The greater the risk, the greater the reward." This is certainly a principle of the kingdom. Those who risked much and even their lives received an eternal reward, as well as honor among men in this world. Just look at the lives of the patriarchs who dared to dream and believe that God would give them something they could not see. Remembering all that Joseph has gone through to this point, it is no wonder God could make him the head of the Egyptian economy: he dared to dream and believe God. He also sacrificed or risked losing the love of his brothers. He could have said nothing and ignored his God-given dreams just to placate his brothers. Many times we compromise what the Lord has told us because we esteem the love and appreciation of those around us more than the will of God. But Joseph was God's faithful servant first.

Because he was faithful to his calling, Joseph risked losing his relationship with his father at a time when he had already lost his mother. Closeness to his father was an important need in Joseph's life. Parental ties keep a continuity of family relationships and help us to identify with our roots. While most of us will begin to experience the loss of parents at a later age, when we have had the chance to mature in our understanding, Joseph encountered the loss of this important relationship at the tender age of 17. What made Joseph's emotions so heightened was that he did not lose his father to death—that is resolvable. He lost access to this relationship because he believed in something that the Lord had told him, which created envy in those around him. It was not so much that he lost someone, as much as it was that someone was *taken from him*. That makes it more difficult to accept.

Joseph also sacrificed the comfort of having a family of his own. He could have remained in Canaan to marry and raise a family. But by believing in his dream, he was forced from the setting where he could pursue this desire. His family became those he was owned by, enslaved to and imprisoned by. From the pit to slavery to prison, this 17-year-old youth sacrificed the things that others so readily claim as a right.

In addition, Joseph left the stability of friendships. Because of his lowly position, he was not allowed the joy of having a good friend. He was a minority in a majority world which, because of his position, did not allow him the normal kind of friendships. Yes, he had favor among his masters, but favor does not necessarily imply friendship. His social standing did not allow those who favored him to fellowship with him as a friend. He was still a servant and a prisoner.

Joseph accomplished all that he did without the power of fellowship with others of his faith. By dwelling in a heathen nation that did not worship the one true and living God, Joseph was forced to sacrifice the power that comes with fellowship with those who call unto God with a pure heart. Fellowship keeps us in the unity of the Spirit, encircled in the bond of peace. It provides camaraderie and companionship, and helps to fortify our spirit with the knowledge that there are others who feel the same way about God that we do. Fellowship strengthens us when we are weak, encourages us when we are discouraged, supports us when we feel abandoned and enlightens us when we lack knowledge. It is one of the greatest advantages that a Christian has. For this reason, the Apostle Paul admonished us to *"Forsake not the assembling of ourselves together, as the manner of some is"* (Hebrews 10:25).

Others who dared to follow God's directives sacrificed much as well. Moses had to flee the comforts of Egypt; David was hunted down like a criminal. Elijah had a death sentence issued on his life. Isaiah ran from his pursuers and hid himself in a log. His pursuers sawed the entire log in half with him in it. Jeremiah was thrown into a hole in the ground, and his book was burned. Peter was crucified upside-down. Stephen was stoned for preaching the Gospel. Antipas, the faithful martyr, was burned at the stake. The stake miraculously burned away from him, so Roman soldiers had to shoot arrows to kill him. John, before being exiled to the island of Patmos, was boiled in oil by the emperor Nero. There in the midst of the boiling oil, John was singing the praises of God. Nero was so afraid of him that he ordered them to pull him out and exile him instead of killing him.

All of these sacrificed some things we consider essential. They risked their very lives for the sake of doing the will of God by following their dream. There is *much to give up* when we dare to dream. The rewards, however, are *exceedingly great!* Those willing to sacrifice will gain access to the presence of the Lord in unique ways.

Genesis 48 gives us some interesting insights into the life of the Israelites in Egypt. Joseph generally resided in the capital city of the country, while his father Jacob stayed in the country of Goshen, well outside of the city. While certainly being in close proximity to his father, he was not always able to get to see him on a regular basis. After all, he was running the entire economy of the most powerful nation on the face of the earth at that time. Even with the best of staff and resources, he could not be far from the center of activity.

When he heard of his father's illness, he immediately took a leave of absence to visit his father. Knowing that his father's departure was imminent, he took his two sons with him. When Jacob learned that his son, Joseph, was coming to see him, he was refreshed. When Joseph arrived, Jacob reminded him of the history of what God had said to him. The restatement of the promise of God to Joseph was a direct sign of Jacob's intention. In this private, intimate moment with the son who possessed the same anointing as he did, Jacob shared the Lord's promise and his desire.

Jacob shared this special moment with Joseph and not with all of his sons. He blessed the two sons of Joseph and claimed them as his own, thereby giving them the right to be counted among the 12 tribes. This unprecedented act sets Joseph apart from his other brothers: not only will he receive a blessing, but his two sons will share equally in the patriarch's blessing with Joseph's own brothers. This special pronouncement brings his grandsons into the covenant of blessing normally reserved for sons.

It is within the God-given power of a father to *bless or curse* his children. Many of our young men are suffering without direction now because their fathers did not know that they had the God-given power to shape and direct their son's future. Part of the privilege of fatherhood is that fathers have the power to speak into the lives of their children what they want to come to pass. They can only do so effectively when they fully understand their God-given power. When they don't understand the power at their disposal, their speaking brings about different results. When fathers are addicted, alcoholic, abusive, unbalanced, turbulent and so out of control that they even have to be incarcerated, they are speaking negative messages to their children and may not even know it. Unless some anointed man steps into the lives of their children, they will be left to the destiny shaped by the voice and actions of their father. Are we, as fathers, handing down blessings or curses? Let us pray that God grant us the grace to hand down blessings only and be understanding if our children display our less admirable traits, encouraging them to do better.

Jacob *blessed* his grandsons, giving them an inheritance that in some cases exceeded that of their uncles. This action set a prophetic precedent for how the land of Canaan would be divided several centuries later. Ephraim and Manasseh would have an inheritance of land along with their father Joseph and his brothers. In blessing them, he set the younger before the elder. This was also unprecedented, as the firstborn always has the right to the inheritance. Joseph was disturbed about this, but Jacob helped him to realize the purpose of God for them both. This was a foreshadowing for how Jacob was going to bless Joseph above his own brothers—the younger being blessed above his elders. It is interesting to note that although the blessing of the firstborn is a Hebrew covenant, none of the patriarchs were firstborn sons. Throughout their history, from Moses and even to David, the rule of the firstborn is not always applicable.

Remember God is still sovereign and can do what He wants to do.

Another possible reason for this switch in blessing might have been because of how the children were named. *Manasseh,* Joseph's firstborn, meant "God made me forget my toil and all my father's house." This name implies that, at the time, Joseph's joy had temporarily made him oblivious to his heritage. He was in Egypt now and running the country. Why would he need to remember where he came from? *Ephraim,* on the other hand, meant that "God hath caused me to be fruitful in the land of my affliction." His reference to Egypt as the "land of his affliction" indicates that his stay might be temporary. The meaning of the names we give our children may prophetically declare their future.

In Genesis 49, we see the blessing of the entire Hebrew clan. Jacob gathered his sons so that he could give them prophetic insight and blessing for their future. In order of their birth, he gives them knowledge of the future judging from how they have lived their lives. Sometimes it is not hard to predict the outcome of people's lives. We can easily see where their actions will lead them. So, just like students awaiting their report cards, who basically know what to expect based on what they have done academically, Jacob's sons have some knowledge as to how their father will speak to them.

In the case of Reuben, Jacob said he was unstable and would not excel. Remember, in the private meeting, he claimed Ephraim (Reuben's nephew) in his place. Reuben had angered his father by laying with his concubine Bilhah, Rachel's handmaid, in Genesis 35:22. This action set him up for the disappointment of missing the blessing of the firstborn.

Jacob next called together Simeon and Levi. Having already given the second son's blessing to Manasseh, he pronounced their future at one time. Their anger against Shechem, whose son, Hamor, had raped their sister, Dinah, after Jacob had made a covenant with them, set them up for their father's pronouncement. Anger and wrath cannot be blessed.

Judah, the fourth son, was the first of the sons to receive a blessing. He is given the blessing of the king. His royal line is the one through which Jesus would come, through another dreamer who sacrificed a great deal and therefore got blessed—his foster father—who was also named Joseph and was likewise the son of Jacob (Matthew 1:16). When given the command to go, Joseph gave up his home in Nazareth to bring Jesus and Mary to live in Egypt (Matthew 1:20). In response to another dream, he then brought Jesus out of Egypt, when Herod had died and it was safe for them to return (Matthew 2:19-20). God used Josephs in both the Old and the New Testaments to bring about His provision in times of particular need in the history of God's people.

Jacob continued down the line sharing with Zebulun, Issachar, Dan, Gad, Asher and Naphtali. After blessing Joseph, he blesses his youngest, Benjamin—the full brother of Joseph and son of Rachel, whom he loved most. But Joseph, the dreamer who paid the price, received the most generous benefit of all: he was blessed with a blessing that exceeded Jacob's forefathers. Joseph's sacrifice paid off. In the private meeting the day before, Jacob had blessed Joseph's two sons as though they were Jacob's own. Among the inheritance of the patriarchs, Joseph now had three portions. In return for the price of being separated from his brothers, he was given a crown upon his head to last forever. He had withstood grief, hatred and envy, and had prevailed. *When we suffer, we will reign! When we take the risk, we will receive the reward! If we are willing to pay the price, we will reap the gain!*

## Chapter Thirteen
# Don't Forget Your Dream

*And Joseph died, and all his brethren, and all that generation. And the children of Israel were fruitful, and increased abundantly, and multiplied, and waxed exceeding mighty; and the land was filled with them. Now there arose up a new king over Egypt, which knew not Joseph* (Exodus 1:6-8).

In Genesis 50:1-26, Joseph buried his father, Jacob, in Canaan and returned to Egypt. He lived to see his grandchildren, who were brought up "on his knees" (verse 23). Before he died, he prophesied to his brothers that God will one day take the children of Israel back to the land of their fathers.

God blesses humanity by placing within each of us His will and purpose for our lives in the form of a dream. When each created human being responds to the call of the Creator and receives His plan of salvation, the gateway is open for that member of creation to show forth God's glory on the earth. When those whom He has touched learn to do what He has called them to do, we see the beauty of God's creation: each joint supplying that which is necessary for the edifying of the entire Body in love (Ephesians 4:7-16).

Each member of the kingdom is important. When we exclude or exile any person that God has anointed, as Joseph's brothers did to him, we leave ourselves with a void we may not have the capacity to fill. Earlier, we saw the components necessary for the effective working of the Body of Christ: dreamers, dream developers, dream managers and dream evaluators. Each is needed for the entire dream of God to come to pass. If one of these gifts is missing, we will not see the full magnitude of what the Lord intended.

When Joseph's brothers threw him into the pit, they were throwing away their blessing. Joseph had three gifts that were critical to their prosperity: the gift of dreams, the gift of interpreting dreams and the gift of management. As the chronicle reveals, these gifts would be expedient to the very lives of Joseph's entire family. His dream would certainly come to pass.

After his family was reunited, the nation of Israel was once again realigned with the full blessing that God had intended. God had brought Jacob down to Egypt to be sustained for the remaining balance of the famine. As the Lord had said, His Word came to pass . . . or had it? After 17 years of provision in the land of Goshen, Jacob dies.

In Genesis 50, an interesting scene unfolds. This great funeral gives some prophetic insights into the future of the children of Israel. Joseph was granted leave, with all of Pharaoh's servants and the elders of the land of Egypt, to go and bury Jacob. Normally, we get about four to seven days off of work for the death of a close relative, but Pharaoh grants Joseph enough time to take his entire family the long distance to Canaan. After the preliminary mourning period in Egypt (70 days), Joseph and the entire nation of Israel return to Canaan to bury their father. They had a great homecoming celebration that lasted seven days.

The homecoming was such a great service that the Canaanites dwelling in the land said that it was a "grievous mourning to the Egyptians" (verse 11). This statement was quite unusual, in that Joseph was mourning for his father Jacob, who was not an Egyptian. Since the Israelites had come from Egypt, the Canaanites naturally assumed they were Egyptian. The Canaanites had not seen God's chosen people for so long that they had forgotten what they looked like. Sometimes, we can become so much like those we live with that we begin to look just like them, sound like them and even act like them.

Joseph and the nation of Israel returned to Egypt after the homecoming services. While on the way, Joseph's brothers send him a message, supposedly from their late father, to "forgive . . . the trespasses of thy brethren. . . ." Even after 17 years, Joseph's brethren still thought that Joseph held something against them. This gesture showed that Joseph's brothers were not reconciled to themselves or their own past.

Joseph had long forgiven them and moved on from this point, but his brothers behaved just as we do sometimes, when we have not learned to forgive ourselves for our past mistakes and fearing punishment. The most challenging obstacle to overcome from the past is often ourselves! We must learn to let go of our own mistakes. If we can't forgive ourselves, then it will be hard for us to forgive others. If we can't forgive others, then the Father in heaven will not be able to forgive us. God first loves us, then we love Him, ourselves and then others as we love ourselves. God first forgives us, we forgive ourselves, and then we forgive others. If we can't forgive and decide to love others, we break the circular flow of God's love and forgiveness.

As we summarize the story, here are the chronological events that took place. Jacob had come to Egypt at the age of 130 and lived there for 17 years. At the age of 56, Joseph buried his father. God allowed Joseph to see three generations after him. He had become a great-grandfather. It must have been quite a blessing for him and his family to experience his gift of wisdom. As he neared death, Joseph casually reminded his brothers that God would bring them back to the land He gave to their fathers. Joseph instructed them to carry his bones with them when they returned. Upon his death, he is embalmed, as is the Egyptian tradition for former diplomatic heads, and is put in a coffin in Egypt. What a sad paradox that the book of beginnings ends with God's chosen people residing and dying outside of the center of God's will.

Joseph's story reminds us of Abraham's walk of faith with God, since Abraham, another dreamer, believed and was blessed abundantly, and was made the "father of many nations." Previously God had spoken to his father, Terah, but Terah "stopped short of the land of Canaan." After Abraham went to his father's house and lived there, in Genesis 12:1-10, God told Abraham to leave his country and go to the place that he would show him. God told him to go into the new land, promising that He would make him a great nation, that all the families of the earth would be blessed. God spoke to Abraham through the Theophanes (the three men) and also in the visions of the night (dreams).

At the age of 75, Abraham took his wife and family into the land of Canaan. Once in the land, the Lord appeared to Abraham at Sechem, in the plain of Moreh, and again stated that He was going to give this land to Abraham's seed. Moving a little east, to Bethel, he built an altar and called upon the name of the Lord. Abraham calls on the Lord at every available opportunity to know the present mind of the Lord for his life. We also need to check in with the Lord often, so that we may be in touch with his vision for our lives.

Abraham continued his journey southward into Egypt to stay for some time, for there was a very grievous famine in the land—a circumstance that should sound familiar. In Genesis 13, Abraham came out of Egypt with great riches and immediately returned to the altar he had built at Bethel, so that he could again call upon the Lord. After Lot decided to separate from Abraham, God spoke to Abraham and told him to look all around in every direction (even the direction that Lot just headed into), for God intended to give him and his seed all the land he could see. He told him to get up and walk around in the land in any direction, for He would certainly give it to him. After walking around his land, he moved his tent to Hebron (the first Hebrew capital) and immediately built an altar. At every available opportunity, Abraham built an altar to communicate with God.

Genesis 14 tells of Lot's capture and Abraham's rescue

of his nephew. It also introduced the practice of *tithing*, or paying a tenth of all that we have received. In Genesis 15, Abraham asked God for a sign that he shall inherit the land as God has promised. Abraham had already lived in the land, but in order for it to be an inheritance, he must have a son there, called by his name. But at this time, he only had his servant with him. While sleeping, God spoke to him in a dream. He told him that his seed would be a stranger in a land that was not his own, and that his descendants would serve the inhabitants of that land. God also related that although this nation would afflict his seed for 400 years, He would bring them out with great substance. He further told Abraham that he would live to be a good old age, and that in the fourth generation, his seed would come home again.

Prophesy is both forthcoming and foretelling. The former sets out what is about to proceed or appear from the mind of God. The latter shows God's viewpoint of circumstances based on what He has seen in our behavior. It predicts what shall happen based on our human characteristics. When God spoke to Abraham about the bondage of his seed, He was not speaking His intention (forthcoming). God was foretelling the future of God's descendants, which was contingent upon their actions. God had noticed an inherent faith deficiency in the family he had chosen to be His special people. First his family, beginning with Terah (Abraham's father), had difficulty leaving the familiar and being separated. Then, when they did move out, they always seemed to stop short of where God told them to go. When faced with famine, which is the test of faithfulness, in the land where they were instructed to be, their first reaction was to run to Egypt, as Abraham would do shortly after this revelation. They always seemed to be unable to settle in the exact place where they where supposed to be. They were always moving on their own because of their lack of faith. As a friend of Abraham, God was giving him insight about the future he saw. God was saying, "Abraham, based on what I see, here is what is going to happen to your descendants." With their relationship being so close, Abraham could have inquired of God as to how to bring about a different outcome.

In Genesis 16-19, we see the birth of Abraham's son by Sarah's maid, Ishmael. We also see his removal from the scene and the manifestation of God's child of promise, Isaac. In Genesis 20, Abraham journeyed a little further south, possibly to find better grazing ground for his cattle, since the Lord had promised to give him the land for an inheritance. Certainly there was nothing wrong with moving his central location when he felt it necessary. He then ran into Abimelech, the Philistine king who tried to take his wife. Similar to the experience in Egypt, Abimelech has a dream where God warns him not to touch this woman. After discourse on this matter with Abraham, Abimelech gave him great riches and even gives Sarah 1,000 pieces of silver for his mistake. Again God proved His covenant to Abraham by increasing his wealth, in spite of Abraham's own fears about who he was and what God had called him to be. Abimelech told Abraham to dwell in any part of his land that he pleased. In this invitation, we see God already fulfilling His promise to give Abraham all of the land he could see.

In Genesis 21, Sarah conceived and bore the child of the promise. But now she also began to despise the child of her handmaid, Hagar. Hagar and Ishmael are forced to leave, but God promised Abraham that He would take care of them, too. Abraham had acquired this woman during his stay in Egypt, but there is no clear record of God telling Abraham to go to Egypt in the first place. Abraham went somewhere the Lord did not tell him to go and came out with someone he should not have had in his life. Sometimes our stay in Egypt can cause us to acquire things that will be a burden to us later on.

Further into Genesis 21, the Philistine king, Abimelech, saw how God blessed this anointed man, Abraham. Abimelech decided to make a covenant of peace with him after reproving Abraham about his herds trespassing onto his property, where he had dug a well. They made a covenant, naming the place *Beersheba* and called on the name of the Lord there. Abraham dwelt in the land of the Philistines for many days.

In Genesis 22, God tested Abraham with the sacrifice of his son. God met him at the point of commitment and provided a ram in the bush to take the place of his son, Isaac. He also reminded Abraham of His promise to multiply his seed and stated that his "seed shall possess the gate of his enemies" (verse 17). He returned to Beersheba, where he heard of his brother and the children with which the Lord has blessed him.

In Genesis 23, Sarah died in Hebron. Abraham purchased a field for her burial from Ephron, a Hittite. Although Ephron offered him the burying place free of charge, Abraham insisted on giving him money for it. Sometimes we can't see when the Lord has given us possession of the land, and we try to buy our way into something we already own.

In Genesis 24, Abraham made his servant promise to find a wife for his son, Isaac, from among his brother Nahor's household and not of the daughters of the Canaanites. It seems that Abraham has learned his lesson about the heathen women in this land. The servant found Rebekah, and she married Isaac. In Genesis 25, Rebekah bears twins, Esau and Jacob. During her difficult pregnancy, the Lord told her that the younger son would rule over the elder. The recurring theme held true with Jacob and Esau, just as Isaac, too, had been blessed above his older brother, Ishmael. Esau despised his birthright because of hunger and sold it to his younger brother, Jacob, for bread and a bowl of beans.

Genesis 26 begins by repeating another common happening in the lives of the patriarchs: There is another famine in the land. God spoke to Isaac in the usual manner and specifically forbade him to go into Egypt. He directed him to dwell in the Philistine land where his father Abraham was known and respected as a prophet and prince. While there, he used the same deception that his father had deemed necessary to use: he told them his wife was his sister. When Abimelech noticed it, he rebuked Isaac and warned all of his people not to touch Rebekah, his wife. The anointing by now should be apparent to Isaac, for God has put the fear of all the nations upon him. As a sign of God's blessing, Isaac sowed in that land and reaped a hundredfold in the same year! After experiencing increase, Isaac went to Beersheba, just as his father had. In this place, the Lord spoke to him again in the usual manner and reminded him of the promise He made to his father Abraham. He built an altar there just as his father did and dug a well for his herds. Abimelech then went to Beersheba to make a covenant with him, as he had done with his father, Abraham. The *anointing* will bring the respect of the heathen around us. The heathen will notice the anointing and blessing of God upon us, sometimes even before we see it.

In the next chapters of Genesis, we see the focus move from Isaac to the next in the patriarchal order, Jacob. Jacob supplanted or stole the blessing of the first-born from his brother Esau. Rebekah then urged him to leave the land to get a wife from his uncle's house. In Genesis 28:10, Jacob left Beersheba to go to *Haran*—where his grandfather Abraham lived until he was 75. While on his journey, he took a rest, and God spoke to him. After the Lord's visitation, he vowed to serve the Lord and placed a stone in the place which he called *Bethel*—where his grandfather Abraham had built an altar to the Lord when he first came into the land. Abraham had also returned there after coming *out of Egypt* with great treasure.

In Genesis 29-32, we see the development of the young patriarch, Jacob, as he dwelt in Padanaram, the land of his uncle, Laban. There he married two women, Rachel and Leah, and fathered 11 children. When it was time to go, the Lord told Jacob in His typical mode of communication to take everything and go. On his return to be reunited with his brother Esau, Jacob wrestled with the angel, who gave him a new name, *Israel*, which means "ruling with God!" No longer was his name to be *Jacob*, which means "deceiver" or "supplanter." When we hold onto our vision and keep the objective in mind—that of returning to the place where God told us to be—He will change our name to reflect His blessing toward us.

In Genesis 33 and 34, Jacob reunited with his brother Esau and brought his family to dwell in Shechem. There his sons, Simeon and Levi, embarrassed him by breaking his covenant with Shechem. When we stop short of where God has told us to go, we can encounter some unexpected misfortune that can hinder the blessing of God. Remember, Abraham's stay in Egypt yielded Hagar, and thus Ishmael, whose descendants are still fighting the descendants of the son of promise, Isaac, to this day.

In Genesis 35, God spoke in a dream to Jacob to go to Bethel and make an altar there, just like he had done when he had fled from Esau. God had to remind Jacob of his promise to Him: to return to Bethel to worship the Lord. When we are in trouble, we will promise God much; when He delivers us, we often forget to render unto Him what we had vowed. In verse five, we see the anointing again caused terror upon those around Jacob, so that no one would dare bother with him or his people. God kept the promise He made to Abraham in Genesis 22:17, that his "seed shall possess the gate of his enemies." God visited Jacob again at Bethel, reminding him of His promise to multiply his seed, that He has changed his name to Israel and that He will give him his seed, the land. Jacob set up a pillar of stone to worship the Lord and gave him an offering. From there, he went to Ephrath, where Rachel died giving birth to Benjamin. He then went to Edar, where his son, Reuben, laid with his concubine. Jacob traveled to Hebron, where his grandfather, Abraham, had lived and his father, Isaac, currently dwelled. While there, Isaac died at the age of 184. Esau and Jacob buried their father, and Jacob stayed in Hebron.

Genesis 36 lists the family of Esau. Many of these children are the predecessors of those whom the children of Israel would have to drive out of the land of Canaan when they returned under Joshua's administration. From living in a land of their blessing, how did they get to a coffin in Egypt?

God called a people into a place to show forth His great power in them. Abraham was the chosen one to bring about God's desire of having a holy nation that would worship Him and show forth His glory among the nations. Through him, God intended to bring about the blessing of mankind. He began by bringing the Hebrew people into a tract of land where he could separate them from all of the ungodly influences around them. During their tenure in the land, God placed His anointing upon them, which caused the peoples in the land to fear them. They prospered with everything they set their hands to do. But whenever they moved outside of their land—the center of God's will—trouble occurred.

As long as Isaac, Abraham's son, dwelt in the land— including the capital city of Hebron, Beersheba, Bethel and the surrounding areas—he was blessed. When there was famine, God specifically forbade him from going down into Egypt, but sent him to the land of the Philistines. There, the fear of God fell upon the Philistines, who willingly yielded to the anointing upon Isaac.

After Jacob, Isaac's son, had fled the land, he was blessed to return with more than he had when he left. But when he stopped short of Bethel, trouble came upon his family. God told him to get in the center of His plan to receive the blessing.

God is always moving his servants, the patriarchs, back to the center of the place from which He desired to raise up His holy nation. Joseph, an anointed part of the plan, lived in Hebron, the place where Abraham and Isaac lived and Jacob resided. When his brothers drove him away, God's plan for the nation went out of balance. Joseph was sold into the very place to which God had told Isaac in a dream never to return. This placement throws a wrench in the plan of God, but since God works all things together for our good, He devised a means that *"his banished be not expelled from him"* (II Samuel 14:14). He used Joseph's gifts to position him at the head of the nation so that he could be a blessing to his entire family.

God told Jacob to go into Egypt, and that He will bring him back. At this point, there were five years of famine remaining. Jacob went to Egypt, and died there after 17 years. They returned to the land they owned, had the funeral and then returned to Egypt. Joseph lived for another 54 years, until the age of 110. During this time, he continued in the service of Pharaoh up until retirement. His people prospered; they were blessed. They got the equivalent of a "welfare check on the first," and received AFDC and food stamps. They lived in Goshen or government-sponsored housing. Joseph, however, lived in what we would call the suburbs. He drove a BMW—the finest chariot in the land—and owned a nice split-level home. He had a government pension and was financially secure, but things were not as God would have them.

Before Jacob came down to Egypt, God told him that he would bring him back home again. Did God lie? Jacob died 17 years later, never having had another dream. At age 30, Joseph interpreted the dream of Pharaoh. For the next 80 years, no dreams or interpretations are recorded in Joseph's life. What happened? God's people got comfortable and forgot their God-given dream, which is where their instructions come from. They forgot to seek the Lord in the gift (the dream) by which He had caused them to prosper. When God told Abraham that his seed would serve under bondage in a strange nation for 400 years, He was not stating His will. He was foretelling what the future would be for His people. The patriarchs had an opportunity to change the future, but forgot to dream and keep in contact with God, who could change the future of their children.

Over time, the mood toward the Hebrew people changed. The Egyptians, who despised shepherds (Genesis 46:34), grew discontent with their presence in the country. After Joseph's death, the next pharaoh was not sensitive to the relationship that had existed between Joseph and the previous pharaohs. All he knew was that the people were multiplying in the land and could present a potential danger if they should align with his enemies. He was intimidated when the young Hebrew men obtained an education, and in spite of almost insurmountable odds, performed at the same level of his own people. His "corporations" cried foul and told Pharaoh that "the most dangerous thing in the world was an educated

Hebrew man." So, he began to deal with them in a subtle manner. First, court cases set a precedent for reverse discrimination. Next, he revoked "affirmative action." Then he redrew congressional districts to limit their representation in the political structure. He then cut spending on "welfare," "Medicare" and "Medicaid," citing that it was the Hebrews' fault that the national budget was out of balance. He put a Hebrew face on Egyptian poverty, which enraged the poor Egyptians in the country, making them think that the Hebrews were the reason for their poverty. The real truth—that the majority of those living off of the people's tax dollars were really Egyptians—was buried under a smokescreen of slanted "media" positions. He began to tolerate the excessive brutality against Hebrew men by Egyptian law enforcement officers, citing that they were the reason for the rash of violent crimes that was causing terror in the cities—even though the true statistics clearly showed that the majority of violent crimes were committed by Egyptians.

He began locking up Hebrew young men for possession of five grams of crack cocaine, while his own children were given probation for 100 times the amount of powdered cocaine. Although his own legal advisory committee recommended that he be fair in the administration of justice, he disregarded their advisement. He began to attack the moral values of the Hebrews as being the cause of the decadence in the society, when the Hebrews were not the owners of television networks, production companies and movie studios that produced the garbage that clouded the minds of the country's youth.

By the time Moses came along 390 years later, the

children of Israel had been in cruel bondage and anguish
of spirit for so long that they did not even remember that
there was another place in which God wanted them to be.
At the age of 40, Moses had a dream of setting his people
free. After 400 years, God finally had a leader who would
be sensitive to His voice. Moses came to his own to help
them, and they rejected him because they did not think
that their deliverance would come from one of their own,
who looked like them. Afraid of being caught, Moses fled
into the land of Midian, where he settled.

But God got his attention again. He renewed Moses'
dream to be a deliverer of His people. On the mountain,
Moses went into a revival meeting that renewed his hopes
in the dream that God had put in his heart some 40 years
earlier. Moses now believed that God had given him the
dream, and whether he was the only one to believe it or
not, he would set forth on an epic journey to deliver mil-
lions of people with a word in his mouth and a rod in his
hand. The people had been so far removed from their
dream that, when Moses led them out, they had no con-
cept of where they were going. The land that they had
owned—the land which Abraham, Isaac, Jacob and
Joseph had lived in—had become to them a *Promised
Land*. They were so out of touch with the Lord and their
heritage that what was once their *possession* now seemed
only a *promise!*

Are we so far away from our God-given dream that it
has now become just a faint promise off in the distance?
Have we lost contact with God in the gift that He has
given us to bless us? Have we stopped looking to Him for

a better way? Maybe we have become like Jacob and Joseph: we have stopped dreaming.

Don't forget your dream! Dreams are what God gives to us and to our children. What we need, like Moses on the mountain, is a revival. In the presence of the Lord, our dreams—our visions for the future—will be revived and restored. So, to awaken the world—God's creation—to the fulfillment of God's purpose, He promised us a revival.

> *And it shall come to pass afterward, that I will pour out my spirit upon all flesh; and your sons and your daughters shall prophesy, your old men shall dream dreams, your young men shall see visions* (Joel 2:28).

When the Spirit comes, we will be quickened, for we were all *born to dream!*